SCALING
THE MOUNTAIN
OF GRIEF

Creating a New Normal Through Loss and Healing

Best Wishes

Audrey

Audrey Stringer

Library and Archives Canada Cataloguing in Publication
Stringer, Audrey, 1950–

ISBN 978-0-9737132-1-3

1. Bereavement- Psychological aspects. 1. Title

Editor: Susan Chilton
Proofreader: Laura Pratt
Cover illustration: Cecile McEachen
Design, Layout and Production: WeMakeBooks.ca

Published by
A String of Hope Inc.

All inquires addressed to:
Audrey Stringer, A String of Hope Inc.
P.O. Box 22037, Sarnia, Ontario, Canada, N7S 6J4

Printed in Canada

Also by Audrey Stringer: *Get Over IT! Surviving Grief to Live Again*

Although the enclosed stories of grief and loss are based on actual experiences, clients' names are fictitious but family and friends' names are real.

DEDICATION

*M*y life has been filled with many gifts and I want to recognize my friend since childhood, Raymond Adey, as a very special blessing. I had the honour of walking alongside Raymond on his final earthly journey. He died on January 8, 2011, in the Dr. Linda Bowring Palliative Care Unit at Bluewater Health in Sarnia, Ontario.

Raymond was a man of substance who lived life to the fullest. He died as he lived, with courage, honesty, openness, humour and grace. Raymond had a smile that could light up a room. He was quiet, unassuming, well grounded and an exceptional family man and friend to all. That did not change in his final days. Raymond talked openly about dying. He accepted it. That facilitated many wonderful, intimate and bittersweet conversations. He gave his family hope and peace in their darkest hours. Storytelling was an essential part of my visits and one week before he died, he gave me a final gift: He asked that I eulogize him at his memorial service. Raymond's legacy will live on in each life that he touched.

I also dedicate this book to my 91-year-old father, Charles Hiscock, who became a widower at 84 and has inspired all who know him as he embodies successful grief work and living with a New Normal. We love you, Dad.

CONTENTS

ACKNOWLEDGMENTS

I would like to thank several important people.

My clients and friends for sharing their stories of loss and granting me the privilege of mentoring them on their bereavement journeys.

Susan Chilton for doing a great job as my editor.

Heidy Lawrance for the book design and layout.

My friend Cecile McEachen for her fantastic cover illustration.

My family and other friends for their continued love, encouragement and support in everything I do.

INTRODUCTION

I believe in dreams. When I don't accomplish my dream, I change my dream.

Sometimes our journeys through life take us to places where we can't imagine ever having a dream again.

In the infancy of your grief journey, you may wonder, "Why have dreams?" You may even tell yourself, "I don't want to dream."

Grief work may well be the hardest work you will ever have to take on. You can do it, though, just as I did.

I chose to face my fears and go through the door of grief rather than around it. I assure you that if you take a shortcut around that metaphorical door, that decision will come back and plague you at a later date.

Have the courage and tenacity to forge ahead and deal with all of your feelings of loss now.

Grief and mourning is a process, not an event. I learned that the hard way.

You will get lots of free advice, most often from people who haven't suffered a significant loss. They do not know the journey. They have not walked the thousands of steps or climbed that formidable mountain. Be gracious and when their turns come, be the teacher.

Listen to your inner self and know that your journey, coupled with life and death experiences, are yours alone and unique to you. Be aware that secondary losses may complicate your journey.

Make *Audrey's 5 As of Healing* your mantra: Acknowledge, Acclimatize, Assimilate, Accept and Affirm. Read and re-read until you have the confidence to believe.

The journal in the second half of this book is yours to bring feelings from the inside to the outside and gently let them go. Sometimes, you will need to do this over and over again. Don't be afraid. Go to the feelings, explore them, be honest and release them.

Hang on to a few of the tips that I offer to give you support, confidence and sustenance. Remember that you will have dreams again but in your timeframe.

I wrote this special poem for you to help you befriend your grief journey.

Read *The Strength and Power of Belief* and believe that you will heal.

Love, hope and peace,

Audrey

SCALING THE MOUNTAIN OF GRIEF

THE POWER AND STRENGTH OF BELIEF

Your eyes speak to me of pain and despair. My breath catches.

You remind me of my pain and sorrow. Myriad emotions sweep past me with a glimpse of your sorrow in tow.

You will suffer deeply, it is certain. Loneliness will overtake you at times and bring you humbly to your knees. You will suffer more if you choose to immerse yourself and become immune to wellness.

Moments of peace will break through those lonely clouds.

Laughter and joy will claim their day.

The roller-coaster ride that you must take will set free the growth and hope to sustain you.

The bittersweet memories you will cherish and behold for endless time will anchor you.

The clouds of despair and loneliness will lift and you will rejoice with tears and laughter to begin anew.

Flowers will smell sweeter, the grass will be greener, and the birds' songs will be cheerier.

This is the gift owned by those of us who love to the fullest and dare to grieve and mourn with abandon and passion.

We must bathe in our sorrow, let it go, and like an old familiar friend, revisit it again and again until we say goodbye.

Your pain and sorrow will blossom in compassion and understanding.

Your new life will be full of blessings and gratitude, coupled with peace.

Stay positive despite the pitfalls.

Dream big and dream small, short and long term.

Invite a friend for dinner.

Join a laughter yoga club.

Take time to reflect.

Use the good dishes.

Fill up your vessel.

Don't try to be the person you were before. You are forever changed.

CHAPTER 1

MY JOURNEY INTO
HOPE AND HEALING

*I*f you are reading this book, you are doing so for a reason. As we embark on this journey together, I want to reassure you that grief work and loss reflection can and will open you up to new experiences and deep personal growth. Please believe, sit back and listen to what I tell you as one who has several times been where you are now, and who has scaled the mountain of grief.

Each one of us has a story and when we hear each other's, we realize we are not so alone. We suddenly feel connected. In doing your grief work, the work called "mourning," it is important to be able to tell your story over and over until you are able to integrate your loss. Sharing it will help you accept it. Bringing dark emotions and pain from inside into the light of the outside and gently letting go is part of your healing process.

I have experienced many challenges, transitions and changes throughout my 60 years, but from a very early age I learned to grow, expand and live my life to its fullest potential. This involved learning how to turn my sorrows into gifts. Death of my loved ones was the biggest of obstacles, but I have trained myself to stay positive despite the pitfalls. I have found meaning and purpose in my life to give me strength and courage. You can, too.

There are worse experiences than death; one of them is being afraid to live. Grief work is the hardest work that I have ever had to do, and I know I won't experience anything more difficult. My son, Steven, my granddaughter, Tate, and my husband, Rhod, all died within a seven-year period. Five years later, my 73-year-old mother died suddenly of food poisoning. One week later, my aunt died of cancer, and the next week my brother-in-law died of a massive heart attack. In between all these significant losses, I lost many other extended family members and good friends.

I found my grief journey more difficult and arduous when deaths were sudden and traumatic. I had to come to terms with the trauma itself before I was able to move on and mourn.

My personal journey through grief was like having a mountain on my back. I was crushed; I was weighed down. My body felt heavy – laden, with a sore neck and shoulders aching from carrying the grief pressing down upon me. I had nausea and stomach upsets and I ranged from suffering constipation to diarrhea. I went to bed exhausted and awoke in the morning exhausted. Forgetfulness was my companion, my concentration was limited and my self-esteem was at an all-time low. Because Steven's death was suicide, I grieved but did not take the time to mourn. When Tate died two years later, just a few precious hours

Rhod was my support system when Steven and Tate died and now I lived alone for the first time in my 48 years. My grief journey was exacerbated by this secondary loss. I was fearful of losing my son, Gavin, and my daughter Lexine to death. I also realized that they feared my death in the wake of their father's. It is natural and normal to feel these emotions of loss, anxiety and impending doom. Losing one significant loved one leaves us fearful of losing others who are important to us.

after her birth, I experienced grief but did not mourn, and I grieved not only for me but for my daughter, too. When Rhod died, I had to do the work of grieving and mourning all three deaths. Only at that point, when I was emotionally, physically, psychologically and spiritually compromised, did I stop, stay suspended and not run from my bereavement journey. I no longer had the strength to run. I gave myself permission to feel and to heal so I was able in the future to live well and love well.

The mountain of grief on my back prevented me from standing up straight for 18 months after Rhod's death. I was often literally brought to my knees in intense pain. The weight of grief was overwhelming at times. I felt as if I had been split down the middle and now half of me was missing. My balance and my equilibrium were off. My memory was compromised, my concentration impaired. At around the 18-month mark, this mountain reduced to a large boulder, and I was able to stand a little taller with a minute amount of confidence. One year later, this large boulder became only a rock, which over time became a pebble. I still sometimes stub my toes on this tiny stone, especially around anniversaries, birthdays and other important days. For me, one week, two weeks, three weeks and even one month leading up to an event are still difficult, and I am emotionally sensitive. On the actual day of the anniversary or birthday, I cope well. You will learn to recognize the onset of these feelings and a sense of dread might deepen your panic and anxiety. At these times, I practice extra self-care. I might book time off work or pamper myself with a massage. I definitely ensure that I am getting ample sleep and proper nutrition and exercise. Learn to listen to "you" and realize that anticipating a special day or event is stressful but know that you will actually cope with it and get through it.

Through the process of writing my first book on loss, *Get Over It! Surviving Grief to Live Again*, I was indeed able to get over my intense pain, and I learned to live with my losses. But I do glimpse and experience similar pain through the eyes of other survivors, and I am sometimes momentarily taken back to my own losses. Then I remind myself that I was at the bottom of the mountain, but I climbed and clawed my way to the top of the mountain. I scaled it. I survived it.

Yes, I stumbled many times and fell many feet to the bottom, but I was determined to heal and live life as I was supposed to. To its fullest. I knew I would have to mourn Steven, Tate and Rhod. They deserved that mourning – and so did I. I needed to mourn. We are sometimes too hard on ourselves, and should lower our expectations of what we can accomplish at a given moment and befriend our grief journey. It will lead us to where we need to be, eventually.

After three significant losses in a short time frame, my grief was overwhelming for the first few months. I didn't want to feel such deep pain anymore. It was torturous. "Make it go away," a plea made by one of my clients, was one to which I could well relate. "When will I stop feeling this pain?" was another question tearfully asked by a bereaved client. My answer was and is, "In your time frame!" Realize that the loss you feel is born out of your attachment to your loved one. We cannot feel the highs of love without enduring the lows of grief. That is the price we pay for loving.

For the most part, the grief journey is one we must go on alone. I can assure you, though, that the pain will ease up as you do your work of mourning. I found meaning

Don't raise the bar too high. You are human! Sometimes, one moment is all that you can deal with; one day may be too much.

You might experience feelings like those that I and many of my clients have: "It is time I am over this intense pain and back to normal." You will discover your time frame, individual to you, and will eventually develop a "new normal." You will be forever changed by the loss of your loved one.

and purpose in my suffering by mentoring others on their bereavement journeys. The intense pain of missing my loved ones did not destroy the hope, strength and joy that I imagined and visualized would one day return. At first, I wasn't able to take one day at a time; it was more one moment or one hour at a time. The resiliency that resides within us is larger than any grief if we believe it to be. We have resources for survival that are hidden until we need them. Tap into these underpinnings and draw on them in your time of need.

I want to create awareness that grief and mourning do not ever go away completely when you love deeply. You will forever remember and feel the sting of grief, at times years down the road in your journey. Grief will lie in wait and pounce when you least expect it to rise up within you. Be patient and let the feelings flow out of you. On the seventeenth and, this year, the eighteenth anniversary of my son's death, I experienced all the same feelings I did on the day he died. This is normal and healthy. Let this life experience become a part of you, but be gentle with yourself and reach out for support during these difficult times.

Sandra was seven years old when her mother died. She is 59 now and still misses her. On Mother's Day, she goes to her photo album, reminisces, shares stories with her children and often places flowers on her mom's gravesite. You never forget and always miss your loved ones.

Let this life experience embrace you and allow this loss experience to shape and mold you. Eventually, growth and strength will be the victors. Do not feel guilty if you do not grieve deeply because you did not love deeply. All rela-

Melanie came to me for counselling because she was happy that her husband Todd had died. She was experiencing anxiety and guilt over what she viewed as an unnatural response as a widow. I learned that Todd was physically and sexually abusive for 22 years. Sandra's life with him had been hell. She now felt a sense of relief; the nightmare was over. She wanted to rebuild and recreate a new life but felt a sense of guilt. In

tionships are different and unique to each of us as human beings. The loss of a beloved pet is very difficult for many people. A beloved friend who died may be more important than a family member who died. Don't let these feelings of grief stop you from loving and living a full life again.

For healing to take place after a significant loss, you must feel the gut-wrenching pain, the overwhelming longing and the desolate loneliness. That is the price of attachment. Let the tears flow and flow, until the river becomes a stream. Delve deep within your being and give yourself permission to "feel." Feel the dire despair, unrelenting ache and seemingly unbearable pain. You must dive deep within your soul, for bereavement work is truly soul work. Grief work can only be done by you, but must be shared with others. Let your emotions surface. This is called mourning. It is a journey we cannot skim over if we are to heal, live and love well again.

When you visit that deep, dark place, set your pain free by expressing your feelings verbally with the comfort of a non-judgmental person. Keeping a journal was one of my healing strategies. Painting on canvas, working with clay, or being at one with nature may be yours. Again, this process is strictly your timeline, and entirely individual to you. Grief is the emotions and feelings associated with the loss of your loved

counselling, she was able to come to terms with her response to her husband's loss. Ultimately, she realized and accepted that it was OK for her not to miss the relationship that she had had with Todd and to stop yearning for a different relationship with him. If we're not attached emotionally, we will not feel loss with the same intensity. And that's all right.

> You may experience many different thoughts and feelings in one minute: anger, denial, guilt, melancholy, betrayal, fear, sadness, loneliness … or conversely, the emptiness may be overwhelming at times. This is the normal reaction to loss. Your loved one has been torn away from you and you are rebelling in pain. Go toward the pain to get through it.

one. Mourning is freeing those feelings and emotions through whatever outlets you choose. I raised the bar for myself by setting the goal of one day writing a book to help others cope and deal with loss. This goal motivated me to record my pain in my journal, daily. This was helpful, especially because I suddenly lived alone. When I awoke in the early morning, my pain at its deepest and darkest, I had my journal to confide in. Certainly there were many times when I didn't feel like expressing myself in this way, but because I had a goal, I forced myself to chronicle my chaotic emotional state.

On your grief journey from the bottom of the mountain to the pinnacle, you may sometimes pause on your path and ask searching questions: "What purpose do I have

Your world has been torn apart with this loss. Express your "why" questions and venture to the deep, dark recesses of your soul. Don't expect to find solutions or answers, but remember that reflecting is vital to healing. Cry if you need to, but don't feel guilty if you are not a "crier." Glance back at your life and see how you reacted to and coped with previous losses. I prayed to my higher power to give me the fortitude to get through each moment. This gave me strength in my darkest days. When my family and friends expressed that they held me in their prayers, I was able to summon even more courage and feel gratitude.

now?" "Why should I go on?" "Is there a loving God?" "Is there a God?" For many of us, the primary question is "How can I go on living without my child/husband/sibling/parent/person who has been so important in my life?" These questions – especially the "why" questions ("Why them?" "Why me?") – are natural and normal. You may or may not find answers. There may be no answers. It is the *exploration* of these questions that is crucial to your healing.

On Tate's sixteenth birthday last year, I reflected and shared with my daughter, Lexine. Had Tate lived, who would she most resemble, would she like sports, would she be a girly-girl or a tomboy? These are natural musings for parents and grandparents. Give yourself permission to explore and when you are ready, to express feelings or wonder aloud about "what could have been."

It is natural for us as humans to want to feel love and to be loved by family and friends. That is our nature, and it gives us a sense of belonging.

We are living longer now and spending more time with one another, so it makes sense that our attachments are stronger. I have clients who are in their seventies who have lost parents in their nineties, and they are devastated when they become orphans. On the other hand, grief is also great if your child died at or closely following birth or through miscarriage. Your future hopes and dreams are gone now. Your vision of what life would be for you and for him or her has passed. Death's timing is never good. Our self-worth may be neatly wrapped up in our spouse, partner, child or parent, and now that person has died. How could this happen? Trust is broken and fear dominates our thoughts. This is normal.

You are forever changed by the death of someone attached to or important in your life. You may, as I did, feel vulnerable, unsafe and insecure. Before the death of your loved one, major decisions were a breeze, but now even minute decisions may overwhelm you. After Rhod died, I found it hugely difficult to make decisions. I would waffle

On your grief journey from the bottom of the mountain to the pinnacle, you may sometimes pause on your path and ask searching questions: "What purpose do I have now?" "Why should I go on?" "Is there a loving God?" "Is there a God?" For many of us, the primary question is "How can I go on living without my child/husband/sibling/parent/person who has been so important in my life?" These questions – especially the "why" questions ("Why them?" "Why me?") – are natural and normal. You may or may not find answers. There may be no answers. It is the exploration of these questions that is crucial to your healing.

Remember that if you love, you will grieve. To heal, you have to feel — give yourself permission. When you accept your journey of grief, your stress will lessen. Don't forget to breathe. Self-care is very important to your well-being. Learn yoga breathing techniques or practice meditation to assist you in your journey. I remember that I would hold my breath for long periods of time and forget to breathe. This resulted

back and forth and question every personal or professional decision I made. Gone were my confidence, self-assuredness and ability to make split-second decisions without looking back.

I reverted to being a small child after my husband died. I needed the safety and comfort of my parents, even though I was 48 years old. I had to learn how to crawl again, and then how to pull myself up and hang onto the coffee table. Like a toddler, I toppled over many times, bumped my head and scratched my knees. This analogy — and my parents — gave me permission to be that youngster once more, to reach out for support and not have to minimize my feelings.

In time, post coffee table, I was able to walk. Years later, I could run again. We can be blindsided by grief and mourning. We aren't aware of the intensity of our feelings until we experience the death of someone meaningful or remarkable in our lives. We can think, imagine and talk about this loss, but only when we walk in the shoes of grief do we experience the turmoil that loss brings. You will have to forge your own individual path. It may be similar to mine, but no two are ever the same. Our thumbprints and footprints are different and unique, as will be our bereavement journeys. Accept the pain, feel the pain, let go of the pain and revisit the pain often, until you are able to integrate it into

in a lot of sighing. When I got in tune with my body and practiced yoga breathing, I didn't feel as overwhelmed or anxious. The oxygen would reach to my brain. Take a grief break. You need the distraction. Leave town for a few hours, go meet a friend in another town. Get out of your environment to clear your head and lessen your dread.

BENEFITS OF DEEP BREATHING: Some changes that your body goes through in response to stress are increased heart rate, narrowing of vision, muscle tension, sweating and hyper-sensory sensitivity. I was a yoga instructor myself, but when I needed self-care, I took classes from another instructor. I told her my story and admitted openly that I needed special attention at that time.

your life as you know it now and will know it. Grieving is not unlike gardening: you must go to the bed, plant new flowers, pull out the weeds, water, fertilize and await new growth.

Life will throw us many curve balls, sunny moments, anguish, pain, joy, wonder, seeming miracles and yet more grief as we experience its many seasons. A key point to remember: We can't control what happens to us, we can only control how we react to those events. Our reactions are what determine or help us on our journey. For me, the more deaths I experienced, the more I was able to accept that death is a major part of our life cycle. We must roll with the punches; they are tragic but inevitable.

Let go of your pride and your fear of rejection or of being the proverbial burden, and allow family and friends to support you through the difficult days. You will have to verbalize your needs of that moment. It is natural for them to feel helpless or inadequate in their attempts to support you. Delegate tasks to task-oriented people, such as helping you with chores, grocery shopping or taking the children for a couple of hours. Save your closest confidantes and best listeners to support you emotionally. Everyone has a role to play as a helper, each one invaluable, but we as the bereaved have to be specific and ask for support. That is our task and we must get over how difficult it can be.

Life is to be lived moment to moment, remembering not to re-live or regret our yesterdays or to go too soon into the future. You may visit the past, but don't linger there, and you may glimpse the future, but don't rush there. Stay in the present, because this precise moment is all we have, all we can be sure of, all we can know right now. This

You will have to reinvent and recreate yourself as a person. You will become someone else as a result of the loss of your loved one. Self-esteem and self-confidence can erode. When you are looking in the mirror, you may not like the image staring back at you. You may experience confusion in your role. "Where do I fit in?" "I am not a wife now!" "I am not a husband!" "I am an orphan!" "My sibling has died." "I only have two children instead of three." "My only child died." Remember that you are still the parent of your deceased child. You are still your mother's daughter. You are still your brother's brother. These roles did not and never will change.

task requires a lot of self-talk. Self-talk is an expression of your pain. You don't need a long-term solution; just acknowledge these immediate feelings and let them go.

Roy did not realize how much he would miss Roseanne when she died. He thought that because she had been ill for three years, he had worked through his grief and mourning. This was the free advice his family and friends gave him. It was partially true: Roy had started grieving the moment Roseanne was given her diagnosis. They had journeyed together throughout her illness. They had understood her prognosis. But Roy was not prepared for the emptiness and loneliness he felt when she died. No one is ever prepared, even when the death is expected. Roy missed his conversations with Roseanne. He missed the intimate moments, the shared decisions and even, toward the end, the shared fears. Now she was physically gone. He missed the caregivers they had come to know in the last months of Roseanne's life. He missed their cheerful patter when times were hard, and their routines.

Stella and Jim were married for 52 years. They met in high school. Jim's family and friends clucked and told him that he should have a fairly easy grief journey after Stella's death. At their advanced age, nature was bound to take its course, they said. They had had a long, happy marriage, they said. He must have expected it, they said. Not true. Jim found himself completely alone and helpless without

Stella. They did not have children, were co-dependent and, in short, were each other's world. His grief journey was difficult but he eventually volunteered at a local hospice and soup kitchen and gained a sense of meaning and purpose. Some couldn't understand why Jim didn't just slow down, but Jim knew why – and that Stella would be proud.

BEACON OF HOPE

Be gentle with yourself as you grieve and mourn. Unresolved loss of the past may rear its ugly head. I grieved and mourned Steven, Tate and Rhod at the same time. Multiple, compounded or delayed grief is harder work, but it is never too late to grieve and mourn someone who has died even much earlier. Circumstances may have stopped you from mourning a previous loss. Perhaps when your husband died, you had three young children, as my client Doris did. She was so, so busy, and everyone told her that she had to be strong for her children. So she diligently put her mourning on hold. She went on with her life and had been remarried for eight years when her brother's wife died. The loss of her sister-in-law, to whom she was very close, unearthed unresolved feelings from the death of her first husband, who died suddenly of a heart attack at 30 years of age. This became her time to mourn him.

One month after Cecile's husband died, her mother died. One year later, her son died. She gave form to her feelings by signing up for a watercolour course. Often, before we come to terms with one significant loss, yet another loved one dies. This I know all too well. It is never too late to mourn. It is important not to minimize your feelings and to recognize the legitimacy of expressing them, no matter how much time has passed.

The importance of finding meaning in suffering cannot be overemphasized. After many months drifting aimlessly in the abyss, finding meaning in suffering gave me a sense of purpose, strength, hope and control. Giving to others creates a sense of self-worth and belonging. This in turn gives us self-confidence and the sure and certain knowledge that we *can* live again without our loved one or ones. You are not the same person now. You are forever changed by the death of your loved one. Your view of the world has been altered, and how others see you has been altered. You are the same person physically, more or less, but inside, your world and sense of self, security and place have been ripped apart. You may be simply going through the motions of existing in this life for months or even years.

When my son Steven died, I decided to become a bereavement counsellor, but before I reached that goal I suffered the loss of my granddaughter, Tate, and then my husband, Rhod. After Rhod's death, I knew I had to pursue my goal so I took an early retirement and went on to accomplish this dream. I actually listened to my voice – my "intuition." In April 2000, on a return trip from visiting my parents on the east coast, a little voice had whispered, "Check to see when you can retire from your current job." When I returned to work that Monday, I went to see the accountant. She told me that on November 1, 2000, the month after my fiftieth birthday, I would be eligible for early retirement.

Within a day, I presented my letter of retirement to the organization. My announcement was greeted with disbelief. One co-worker asked, "Why are you retiring at your age?" Another demanded, "What are you going to do with your time?" "You will get depressed," others warned, ominously. I held my head high and told them, "I am going to follow my dream!"

I have only one life to live and I was determined to re-create myself. I believed that I had a gift to offer others and I planned to turn my sorrows into gifts.

Volunteer at a soup kitchen, or school breakfast program, or visit a senior to take a grief break. The gift of your time and caring for others will give you a sense of meaning and purpose despite your inner turmoil. Sometimes, you need to just step away and take a breather from grief and mourning, and this is a healthy, helpful distraction. Join a support group at your local hospice, church or funeral home, or if you're not quite ready for face-to-face interaction, join a bereavement group online. Take baby steps to healing. Make a plan to scale that mountain at your own pace. Mountains to boulders, boulders to rocks, rocks to pebbles... I urge you to choose to survive and thrive rather than be a victim.

Don't cling to the wreckage of your loss. Read this book, investigate resources on grief and bereavement, attend support groups and seek out a mentor who has been in a situation similar to yours, because as hard as it might be to imagine, you do know or will quickly meet such a person. They will want to be there for you, as I do.

Sometimes, the trite is true: You are not alone. There are others who have been there or who are even there right now. We learn how to grieve and mourn together. We can come to grips with our deep, all-over-the-map emotions. You're looking up at that mountain, and that mountain can be conquered.

How did I reach the top of the mountain? Allow me to be your guide and I will show you the way. I trust that you will take away some tips, and will look to my story as a beacon of hope. I can help you cope and heal through your loss or losses. This is my experience as well as the experience of the hundreds of bereaved whom I had the privilege of walking beside and mentoring. These special bereaved people gave me strength and hope with their stories. This book can't be all-encompassing, but it will give you proof that you will survive and thrive *if you make that your choice.* You will come to believe that loss can be empowering.

CHAPTER 2

GETTING THE NEWS

LIVING YOUR WORST NIGHTMARE

*T*he death of someone important to you can catapult you into a nightmare from which you just want to wake up. It is simply too horrible to be true. This surreal, nightmarish feeling may well last for months or longer. Remember: this experience is unique to you. I continually emphasize this point because we have a tendency to compare ourselves to others. Societal pressures coupled with the expectations of family and friends can increase our stress. If you don't "snap out of it," you can feel inadequate, insecure and sometimes like a failure. Don't beat yourself up! Your time frame for grief and mourning is yours and yours alone.

I often say, "thank God for shock," and those of you who have been through a sudden or traumatic loss in particular know exactly what I mean. I probably would have died myself if I hadn't stayed in this suspended state for months.

I still went through the motions and tried to act normally when Steven and Tate died, but I felt as if someone else was in charge of my actions, prompting me to cope with planning and get through the funerals. Some people describe this as being almost an out-of-body experience, like they're watching themselves move and speak, but are not connected to what they are apparently doing.

I was in this state of shock for many months after the deaths of my loved ones. When Rhod died, I was depleted emotionally, psychologically, spiritually and physically. My blood pressure was so low that my physician encouraged me to increase my salt intake. I was prone to lung and eye infections for more than a year after his death. My doctor also suggested antidepressants and sleeping aids. I refused and told him that I was going to go though my grief journey the more difficult way: through the pain, not around the pain. I could not be fixed. I wasn't broken. I wasn't depressed. I was grieving!

It is OK to let yourself feel numb for awhile. This is nature's way of helping us cope with our losses. Don't medicate yourself, because you are only suppressing and delaying your feelings and putting your grief on hold. However, if you were on antidepressants or anti-anxiety meds prior to the death of your loved one, don't make any changes now. If you had trouble with your sleeping patterns before the death of your loved one, you will experience more problems now. If, before he or she died, you were accustomed to waking up during the night, you may feel intense pain and loneliness when you do so now.

When you wake up in those dark hours now, you may be overwhelmed by feelings of loss. Go with these feelings and accept them. See your family doctor a few weeks after the death of your loved one for a checkup.

With the loss of my husband, I knew that I had to mourn my son and my granddaughter, too. I couldn't place my feelings for Rhod, Steven and Tate on a shelf anymore. I knew I wanted and needed to be the care receiver rather than the caregiver for now. My role had been to support and give to others, but I was aware I could no longer do this, nor did I desire to. I had to teach others around me to do this because my role had not changed in their eyes.

I had returned to work two weeks after Steven died. I wasn't ready so I just floated through those days. I was told I was doing a stellar job but I knew someone else was in my body performing those work tasks. I went back to work two-and-a-half weeks after Tate died, too, primarily because I had booked two weeks of holidays and was given three days of bereavement leave. As it turned out, it was not much of a "vacation." Again, though, in what I recognized as going through the motions, I was able to execute my duties to positive reviews.

It was a different story when Rhod died. I was depleted emotionally, physically and spiritually. I couldn't and didn't want to go back to work despite some pressure to return, probably because I had done so effectively in the past. And there are also supervisors and managers who genuinely believe it's best for the bereaved to get back into the thick of things, rather than sit at home and brood. This time, however, I could barely survive a moment let alone a full day. I realized that, with this third devastating blow, I also had to mourn the two earlier deaths I had "worked through" literally, not spiritually.

I was suspended in a world that revolved around me. I couldn't believe this was happening to me again! I lost all sense of time and place; my whole world was upside down.

I appeared the same on the outside, but I was not at all the same on the inside. I had always been a morning person. I had always been conscious of the way I dressed and took pride in my personal care. So I arose early every day and went through the motions of selecting clothing, applying make-up and styling my hair... My habits did not change in the least.

But I was exhausted all the time. I went to bed exhausted and got up exhausted. I was numb, yet in a nightmare that I couldn't escape. I travelled from my supposedly real world to an unreal foreign world, without a destination. Months after the shock wore off, I wasn't prepared for the pain. It was deep, gut-wrenching, visceral pain that took my breath away, carved a huge hole within me, and clawed at my heart. I had never before experienced anything like it. I reeled and struggled against it, pushing it away. It was only when I decided to embrace the pain of loss that I was able to accept the deaths of my loved ones.

By entering into your pain, you will be able to feel it and then let it go. Remember that this is a process, not a one-time event. And remember that this is your timeline, so don't rush yourself. Don't listen to others' experiences or admonitions, or compare yourself to them; just listen to you. Know that the pain will change and lessen. It will evolve and abate, but it will only do so if you share it. If you repress or stuff down your feelings of mourning and don't release them, you will have to face the pain down the road when you suffer another significant loss, as I did.

I assure you that you will not forget your loved ones as your pain recedes or becomes tolerable. Your memories of your deceased loved ones will in fact sharpen. You will be able to "bear" to picture them, hear them and relive your memories with them.

Shock may cushion you for months or years. Your grief journey is yours and yours alone. Reach out for support, though. Lean on at least three good friends who are patient, good listeners, who will not rush you through your grief or try to minimize it. Avoid judgmental and self-absorbed family members and friends when you are feeling low and vulnerable. Know what – and who – you can handle, on a daily basis.

BEACON OF HOPE

I have only vague memories of Steven, Tate and Rhod's funerals, but I clearly recall acting like the "hostess with the mostest." I remember greeting everyone with a smile or a hug and thanking them for coming. I recall politely inquiring after their lives and family members. Was this a funeral or a wedding? If people, including myself, didn't recognize that I was grieving, who could blame them?

The purpose of a funeral or memorial service may be to "celebrate a life," but it is also, I now know, to facilitate your grief journey. Through the very ritual, you are relaying to your family and friends that you need support. You are reaching out to the community for that support. It was necessary for me to have two visitations for each of my loved ones, along with funerals and graveside ceremonies, to feel that the deaths were real and not imaginary. I needed this process derived from my culture and history to keep me grounded.

A family friend questioned us having a church funeral for our son Steven, because his death was suicide. I told her that my God is a loving, forgiving and welcoming God. Ignore all the free advice and do whatever helps you heal. Implement old rituals or develop new ones to suit your needs. Funerals and memorials are for the living and are important to our healing. When our voice can't give words to our feelings, we need ceremonies and rituals to help express and give meaning to our loss.

People will unintentionally hurt you. Some may say, "This is God's will," "God will only give you what you can bear," "You have other children," or, as at Rhod's funeral, "You are young, you are attractive, you will get married again." I wanted to scream at these people or physically slap them. Forgive them or their thoughtlessness will eat you up. I was able to forgive but I certainly did not forget these words and their sting. We can only bring about change within ourselves, not others around us. We can educate but cannot change their mindsets. Use your good energy to heal and don't waste energy on things beyond your control.

My mother Irene was a special lady in my life. We had a wonderful relationship despite the 2,000 miles that separated our homes. When Rhod died, she telephoned me every single day for one full year. When she died suddenly, on November 26, 2003, my world stopped again. She had been healthy and vibrant; who dies of food poisoning in North America? And from a church turkey dinner, no less! I still miss her immensely. Here's an example: I have a shoe fetish. Whenever I buy a new pair of shoes, I think of my mom. On my frequent visits, she would admire my shoes and I would give them to her. Now, when I visit my dad, I long to give her a pair of my shoes, but that is not to be. Instead, I say to Dad, "Mom would adore these shoes!" We chuckle, then share stories about her.

Don't fear that you will forget your loved one. As I mentioned, your memories will become sharper as time goes on. I still miss favourite foods that Mom would prepare for me when I visited. No one makes soups and bread quite the same way and I recognize that no one ever will. That's all right; it's good, in fact. Indulge in the bittersweet memories and share them with others.

On the first anniversary of my mother's death, we gathered as a family for dinner. The tension in the room was so thick we could have cut it with a knife. Seventeen relatives were there. Each of us was thinking of Mom but no one mentioned her name. I decided to start a new tradition and suggested that we each share a memory of her. Faces fell and you could have heard a pin drop in the room. After the second person shared a memory, the tension lifted; after the third, it left. We learned more about Mom through the power of storytelling and each other's experiences. It was a cathartic and beautiful experience we all treasure. My 84-year-old dad beamed from ear to ear, relishing the anecdotes and replaying conversations. Many people had many different relationships and interactions with our deceased loved ones. The sharing of stories takes courage and tenacity, but it's helpful to everyone's healing journey.

Mom loved her flower garden. The year she died, her flowers bloomed at their most colourful and fragrant in years. Since then, my dad, who is now 91, lovingly tends to her garden. He finds enjoyment and healing there and annually plants new flowers.

EXAMPLE:

A client of mine had two grandchildren who were three and five years old when their grandpa died. She used the ritual of lighting a candle at Christmas dinner and sharing memories of him. When the children were visiting, they would often say, "Grandma, let's light a candle for Grandpa," or, "I want to talk about Grandpa." They cherished him through the memories and stories of others. Remember: Children are afraid of what they don't know, not of what they do know.

When my grandchildren's paternal grandfather Poppa Kelch died, they planted pansies in the garden in his memory. It is important for children to be part of the rituals of funerals or memorial services. When words are difficult, use ritual to help break the ice and open the conversation.

Eight-year-old Robin thought her mom did not love her dad after he died. Why? Because her mom did not talk about her dad. Her mom immediately got rid of all of his personal belongings and did not have any photos or mementoes of Robin's dad on display. It was as if he had never existed. Robin cried silently in her room. She began to feel resentful and angry at her mom. In counselling, Robin expressed her feelings and I was able to facilitate a dialogue with her mom. As it turned out, Robin's mom cried in silence, too. She had put away photos in an effort to protect her daughter from the pain she herself was feeling. When they shared pain and hurt, though, the two became much closer and, over time, came to talk and share stories openly.

CHAPTER 3

THE CHAOS OF GRIEF AND MOURNING

Grief is your reaction to the death of your loved one, and mourning is publicly expressing those feelings of loss. Your heart is broken because you loved and were attached to this person. This may be your first experience of losing a loved one. Your loved one may have been torn from you suddenly through a motor vehicle accident, suicide, workplace tragedy, homicide or heart attack. Your loved one may have been ill for several years. Your loss is yours, unique to you, because of your special relationship with that person. Your bereavement journey will be unique to you, and the journeys of others who suffered the loss of the same person will be unique to them.

Even in families, we will not all be on the same page when going through grief. You may be very social and out-going but your brother may be quiet and intense. So it makes sense that your mourning styles will be different. If there were problems with dynamics before the death, these problems may be exacerbated now. Feelings are often intensified by loss. No matter how close you are to your family, you may still feel that you are alone in the world. This is normal. I often felt alone in a crowded room. I often felt alone when I was being hugged!

Look after your special needs now, for you are what I consider a "special needs" person at this time. This death may set you on a downward spiral into a big, dark hole out of which you fear you will not be able to clamber. At times, you may feel like you do not even want to clamber out. Sometimes, when we're exhausted, it's easier to wallow.

Believe me, though: You will be able to lift yourself out of that abyss and scale that mountain.

You may re-experience, re-see and re-feel your loved one's last days. If the death was not peaceful but rather a result of trauma, these images, imaginary or otherwise, may haunt your psyche for months or years. I re-lived every procedure and test that Rhod underwent while in an induced coma for 30 days before we took him off life support. I imagined Steven's final days before he took his life on August 25, 1992. This is normal.

Liz's daughter, Sheila, died of suicide at the age of 32, leaving two beautiful young daughters, aged three and six. Sheila was a high achiever who appeared to have a happy life and a great relationship with her family. One year later, Liz still tries to figure out why her daughter died and beats herself up emotionally on a daily basis. There may be no answers to the "why" questions but we still need to explore them, to gradually usher our feelings from inside to out-

Jealousy between siblings, or sibling rivalry, is commonplace before a death and often magnified after a death.

side and to gently let them go. Releasing them is a process and you will need to consciously work at it until you are able to integrate it in your heart, mind and soul.

This takes huge amounts of energy that you don't have right now. Seek the guidance of a counsellor to help facilitate these very normal feelings.

Willow was jealous of the relationship she imagined her sister Dale had with their mother. Willow married one year after their mom died. She was resentful that their mom had been alive, well and in attendance at Dale's wedding three years earlier. Their mother had been able to meet and spend time with Dale's child, August, and Willow would never have that opportunity. Once her feelings were validated in counselling where they were not judged, she was able to discuss her feelings of loss with her sister and stop viewing her as a rival.

Brianna's husband was killed in a workplace tragedy five years ago. She told me that only now is she able to grieve and mourn him. Since his death, she has made many court appearances. His workplace had been charged, she had to deal with the Workplace Safety and Insurance Board, there had been hearings and meetings, the media were involved … She placed her feelings on hold until the

My dad wailed like a wounded animal and sobbed loudly at the visitation for my mom. In between his wailing and sobbing, he recited the 23rd Psalm: "The Lord is my Shepherd, I shall not want." He clutched Mom's casket with his frail hands and railed in disbelief. Two of my brothers approached me with fear on their faces and suggested that I take him to the doctor. "Look at him! He has completely lost it! He needs medication!" I calmly placed my hand on my brother Everett's shoulder and said, "It's OK. Dad is doing what is called 'mourning,' which means going public with his feelings. He will be fine; just leave him alone and be calm."

case was completed. She worked hard to understand all the proceedings and to represent her late spouse with a clear and focused mind. Her friends and family, however, don't understand that it is only now that she is able to mourn her husband. Five years have passed; their expectation is that she has moved forward and on. She is teaching everyone that she is only now starting her bereavement journey.

We had never seen our dad cry before. My brothers' concern was natural – but so are the crying, sobbing, wailing and releasing feelings. In some cultures, this kind of keening, or even occasions in which survivors physically hurt themselves, is the norm. Look to your family of origin to see how your relatives have coped with previous losses. You won't get a medal for being strong or stoic, even if you have been socialized to keep your feelings in check. Give yourself license to do whatever feels best for you. My mom was the glue that held our family of ten together. This of course changed at the moment of her death.

Who would have thought my dad, who depended on my mom, would not only survive but thrive. At 91, he does his own banking and goes out shopping. When Mom was alive, these were her roles and he was happy to let them be hers. Out of the chaos, he became independent and took on new challenges. He lives life to the fullest. He certainly could have delegated these responsibilities to other family members, but he chose not to. He chose to grow. He chose to thrive and survive. The tasks gave him a sense of control, meaning, purpose and youth that belie his age.

BEACON OF HOPE

It is important to respect and be gentle with each other as you grieve and mourn the loss of your loved one. We tend to want to "fix" each other as we embark on our bereavement journeys. Don't compare or try to change what other family members are experiencing after the death of your mutual loved one. Just accept and don't judge! There is no right or wrong way to grieve and mourn, just our own individual paths of coping and healing. Give each other space but do look for opportunities to share; those will arise in your grief journeys, believe me.

I remember Dorothy Johnson, a palliative volunteer in an organization from Forest, Ontario. She gave me a butterfly pin for my lapel when my son, Steven, died. She told me to wear this pin for comfort until I was ready to pass it on to someone else who had suffered a loss. I wore it for more than a year, then when my friend Carol's mother died, I gave it to her and told her the story. When she went back to visit her father in Ireland a year later, she gave the pin to him. I had the opportunity to visit her dad and viewed the pin placed above the headboard of his bed. He told me that he had found comfort in this symbol. When he died, Carol retrieved the pin and wore it again. Later, she passed it on to another grieving person. The pin is still bringing comfort to the bereaved. This is a legacy of Mrs. Johnson and I reflect on it often.

On Steven's birthday, September 28, 1992, less than a month after his death, many of his good friends decided they wanted to gather for a celebration of his life. One of them, Carol, telephoned and asked what we thought of their plan. Our family was honoured and grateful that Steven had touched so many lives. We knew that these people grieved and mourned his loss, too. We invited them to hold the celebration at our home. Several friends arrived with a tall, skinny maple tree and everyone shared in the planting of this tree in our backyard on that beautiful Sunday. This brought his friends comfort and they needed a place to mourn and share memories of Steven. This maple tree has brought me comfort and sadness as I grieve through each season. The fullness of its green branches in the spring and summer, the changing, vibrant red colour in autumn, and the desolate, empty branches in winter are bittersweet for me as I view this living monument daily from my kitchen window. I have watched this tree grow and practically take over our backyard. It is beautiful, just like our son.

Find comfort in what helps you cope and deal with loss. You can create new rituals that are meaningful for you and your family and friends.

CHAPTER 4

FINDING YOUR WAY TO THE TOP OF THE MOUNTAIN

*F*inding the way up grief's steep slopes may be more arduous and difficult than you had ever imagined.

We live in a society in which illness, aging and death are considered almost shameful. We don't want to face our own mortality. "Forever young!" is the media message in magazines and on TV. The reality is that no one will get out of this life alive. Once we face that inevitable fact, we can really live to the fullest and accept that death is part of a natural cycle. Then we can deal with the experiences – painful and wonderful – that life brings us. My early experiences with death taught me that life is fragile and fleeting, but they never truly prepared me for the death of my closest loved ones. I truly believe that we need to discuss death and dying to normalize it because we will all experience loss one day.

Don't take shortcuts with your rituals when your loved ones die. The funeral and memorial rituals facilitate your grief and mourning process, and help you to acknowledge that your loved one has, in fact, died. If you dispense with these rituals, the message you may be giving family, friends and community members is that you don't require support during this devastating time. Again, look to your past cultural funeral traditions and develop new ones personal to you and your family. Even if you are someone who has scoffed at or shunned visitations before, don't be embarrassed to host one. You now know why others before you have chosen to do so.

Funeral visitations and funeral or memorial services can be physically, emotionally and spiritually draining, but they are necessary to your healing journey. Let's not minimize graveside rituals, either. At times when words are not enough, use the power of ritual, whatever form that may take. Years after Rhod's death, I finally summoned the courage to re-read old cards and notes he had sent me. With Steven, I kept many pieces of artwork, schoolwork and some of his books. I still look at these items and remember. These rituals bring me some peace and comfort.

You have to step backward before you move forward.

BEACON OF HOPE

You may not be able to discard your loved one's belongings because you feel that that is somehow letting go of her or him. Or perhaps you find it too painful to go to the closet or workshop. That is just fine. Do the tasks only when you are ready. It took me a year before I could dispose of Rhod's cloth- ing. I gave some items to family and friends and the rest to local charities. It was a gradual process. His scent lingered on his wardrobe for a long time. There were so many memories attached to his shirts, jeans and jackets ... I was afraid of forgetting him. But I haven't in the least. Quite the opposite.

It is OK to memorialize your loved ones. We have a bench in our local park where we all find great comfort. We also have Steven, Tate and Rhod's names on a wall in another nearby park. Some people choose to start up charities, fundraisers or awareness campaigns in their loved ones' names. Rick and Mavis's daughter died at age 18. They organized a bursary in her name at her high school. This memorial is painful and bittersweet, yet each year when it's awarded they find meaning and a sense of her living on, not only in their memories, but also in those of her community.

Your loved one may have been cremated and you now keep the cremains on a shelf or mantel at home. You might wear some in a locket around your neck. The cremains may even still be at the funeral home. Sidestepping a burial may stop you from moving forward. When my friend Mary's husband died, she went to their home country and spread his cremains in the ocean. She regrets not having a plot in the cemetery here that she, her children and grandchildren could visit if they wished. Josephine took her husband's cremains with her in the car when she drove to the grocery store or bank. He was still alive to her. This was her first death loss in her 50 years. She was stuck in her grief journey and couldn't move forward. With the guidance of a counsellor, she was able to follow through with the ritual of burial and, in time, grieved, mourned and accepted her loss.

Grief and mourning work demand a depth of courage and tenacity that we often don't feel we possess or have access to. I know that we do. I know that you do. Just believe!

Candy went back to work two weeks after her son died. After two hours, she went back home. In her eyes, she was a failure because everyone around her had told her that she needed to get back to the old routine, the "keep busy and you won't be sad" routine. Not only had her routine changed, but her whole world as she knew it had changed. She needed to hear someone normalize what she was experiencing, so she came to me for counselling. Two months later, she was able to resume work but she took Fridays off for the next six months. Fridays were dedicated to her self-care regime. Many people wanted her to return to what they saw as "normal;" in other words, the way she was before her son's death. That was not to be. She has had to develop a "new normal" without her son. It took energy and stamina to educate her family and friends that she will always grieve and mourn her beloved son.

When I realized that I had a big mountain to scale before I could heal, I knew that I had to formulate a plan and write a new set of goals and dreams. This was no easy task and the path was impassable at times. Sometimes, the battle raging within me was "Should I continue to pull myself up from the depths of despair or should I lie curled up in a ball?"

How could I dare think about attempting the former in my darkest days? I decided to let myself face the dark days, but not too many all at once. While there, I experienced questions such as, "Where do I belong?" "How will I fit in?" "Do I have a future now?" "Are all my hopes and dreams dead, too?" If I let myself stay at the bottom of the mountain too long, I would not have had the courage to even dream about reaching the top. I kept reminding myself that I am a survivor.

I committed to a plan to write a book, not just about my losses but about my healing.

I started with the idea of keeping a journal but gave myself the bigger plan of one day writing a book.

I was what we call a "professional caregiver," and this role did not change with the deaths of my own loved ones. The expectation of those around me was: "You are so strong!" "Your losses are going to help you in your work of palliative and bereavement care." Platitudes such as "In the end, death was a blessing," or "God only takes the best" made me want to slap these "fix-me" people. All I wanted was for them to listen and let me tell my story without placating me or making me defend my grief and mourning.

My journal listened and did not judge. When I awoke at two or three in the morning and felt overwhelming loneliness and anguish, I committed those feelings to paper. I took the pain from inside and wrote daily for two years. The secret to journaling is to write but not read your words. Take those feelings from inside, write them in their rawest form and do not think twice or edit. Just turn the page. Reading what you have written will stop you from writing again. You don't want to feel your pain twice in close succession. Feeling it that acutely once is more than enough to bear.

I was a private person whose role had always been as caregiver, not care-receiver. Even though after three losses that sent me reeling I needed lots of support, it was difficult to reach out and ask, let alone accept. The perception of me as caregiver therefore did not change in people's eyes. I found it difficult and draining when I was in public doing banking or grocery shopping.

Someone I knew would stop and ask me how I was doing, but before I had a chance to answer I heard all of their problems. I couldn't handle it. I began to plan my errands around slower times at the grocery store or bank. At other times, when my energy was low, I knew that I could not be around people at all because it would suck me dry. Be aware of your personality type and tolerance level. They may determine your support system and activities.

Again, because I was a private person, I found it difficult to tell my story. I went to a counsellor when my son died, but when the given hour was up, I felt no relief from my pain. I needed more than one hour before I was able or willing to share my pain. In my family, I had been socialized to keep my feelings inside.

You might minimize your feelings, too. Jen would always compare her loss to what was happening in the world. "I should be thankful that I wasn't in a tsunami!" "Thank the Lord I'm not in Haiti!" "Look at Wanda; her husband and son died within the same year and she got through." Jen would shut down her feelings and stop herself from mourning her loss.

Own your feelings, express them and let them go. It is acceptable and even commendable to feel empathy for the rest of the world, but be aware that in doing so you may minimize your own legitimate right to despair and grief.

I must be honest and say that it takes a lot of self-talk and motivation to want scale the mountain of grief. I'll also admit that you'll never be the same. You'll be someone forever changed, but someone who is also renewed.

In your dark days or hours, cling to a vestige of hope, however small it might seem. Hope is what we grab onto to survive, then it grows into the belief that things that are positive are "yet to be for me." I experienced many moments when I tried to imagine a new life but couldn't. I worried about my other children and my grandchildren, and that they would die too. When these negative thoughts descended upon me, I pushed them away because I wanted the word "hope" foremost in my mind.

I thought and said "hope" aloud over and over again until I believed that I had a future without my deceased loved ones. I also realized that we are never prepared for what lies ahead. When my mom died, I toppled back to the bottom of the mountain and I had to climb back up again. There will be many losses in our lives – that, we can't control. All we can control is how we react and cope and that will determine our healing.

When Mom died, I had to take time off before I resumed writing my book. My dad, who was then 84 and visiting me, gave me the inspiration and courage to complete and publish *Get Over It*. I felt guilty that Mom did not have the opportunity to read the final copy. During Dad's stay, I gave him the chapter "Building a Supportive Network" to read. I left the room and when I returned, he was crying. He said, "Audrey, you will help many, many people with this book!" That gave me the will to continue and deep within I found the strength to create and rebuild a new life, now without my mom.

The changing seasons affected my mood and my spirit. Spring with its new life and promise, summer with its light and lushness, autumn with its blaze of colour, and the dreaded winter with its dearth of light and life. I experienced feelings to which I had never been subjected before my losses. I was more aware of and more sensitive to my surroundings and environment. You may experience many

different feelings and sometimes a confusing confluence of these feelings at
the same time. Because you are vulnerable, you may wonder: "What is wrong
with me? I should be at Point B in my

Let the tears flow and
in time you may cry
less often but with
more intensity.

grief journey when I feel I am only at Point A." Don't beat
yourself up. Go with the feelings because, like me, you may
experience the roller-coaster ride that can come with sea-
sonal change.

I do know that several seasons passed before I experienced a sense of joy again.

I cried so much that I thought I would not have any
tears left. There were times when I was sick of crying.
Somehow, I always had tears, but over time, my body, mind
and soul calmed down.

You may experience what I call "grief surges." A
favourite song on the radio, the familiar scent of your
spouse's perfume or aftershave, or an infant crying may set

you off to bawling like a baby, too.

You may glimpse a young man or woman in a crowd who reminds you of your deceased child. I remember seeing a young man that resembled my Steven; my heart skipped a beat and for one long second, I believed it *was* Steven. This is normal and part of wishing and longing in bereavement. I also remember waking up one morning, about 18 months after Rhod's death. The sun was brighter, the birds were singing and the scent of the flowers in my backyard was stronger. It was as if my senses had awakened from a deep slumber, much like a bear awakening from hibernation. My world had stopped, but the world had gone on around me. I started to experience and feel renewal and rebirth. It is difficult to explain to people who have not walked this path or had a reawakening. But when it happens – and it will – you will know.

BEACON OF HOPE

Your loved one's death has left a void around you, and, sometimes, around the whole community where he or she grew up, lived and worked. One life touches so many people. I experienced this at my loved ones' funerals, and it was very comforting. Mrs. Jackson came up to me and told me what a nice young man my son was. He had been to her home and planned on doing some maintenance for her. She met him only once but was touched by his gentleness and warmth. She showed her respect by coming to one of the visitations at the funeral home. This type of unexpected story about my son, from so many people I had not met or even heard about, gave me comfort and hope many times in the years after his death.

I visited the cemetery daily for several years after my loved ones died. I no longer feel a need to go as often. I tend to go once every several months on holidays, birthdays and other dates that were special to us.

Through the rituals of funeral and memorial services, you will learn how much your loved one touched the lives of others. The power of storytelling and the sharing of memories will bring you a sense of peace in your dark days. I remember my Aunt Maggie's funeral. My dad lifted me up to see her in her casket. It was natural, comforting and not scary, though I was but a child of seven. I recalled my grandmother telling me that "funerals are for the living, not the dead." She was very wise because the rituals of funerals and memorial services facilitate your grief journey as you tell your community that you need support. That is the support that will help you in your loss. That is the support that can be ongoing and invaluable long after the fact.

Follow through with the graveside service, though it can be difficult, because this truly is your loved one's final earthly journey. Go and bid them farewell. Gently place a handful of dirt on the casket and flowers on the grave. By taking part in these rituals, you are facing and embracing the pain of loss. You will come through the other side richer, able to celebrate a fuller and healthier life. If funerals such as this are not part of your cultural tradition, participate in whatever yours is. If you don't have traditions per se, create your own to help you cope and heal.

Ken went to the cemetery daily for two years after his wife Shauna died. His family and friends made him feel as if these regular visits were morbid and that he was not dealing with his loss and moving on. Remember that if you have a need to visit the cemetery or mausoleum, it is your choice and should not be judged. Conversely, if you do not feel comfortable going, that is just fine, too. Listen to and heed your needs.

CHAPTER 5

CLINGING TO THE WRECKAGE — FEAR FACTOR

You may be feeling that you are at the bottom of a deep pit or steep mountain and are now trying to claw your way up its slopes. You may be feeling too defeated to even try. "What do I have to live for now?" "I can't go on!" You may vacillate between wanting to survive and wanting to give it all up and join your loved one. This is very painful and at times overwhelming. You have lost your joy, and your zest for living is completely or often absent.

In addition to learning to share these fluctuating feelings with others, I had to learn other new skills to cope.

One of them was trying to live in the moment. In a sense, I didn't have much choice; I couldn't envision the future because I did not see one in the early months of my grief journey.

There may be times when you feel a little strength and then the next minute, you feel weak as a kitten. Grief may roll over you in waves. Or it can suddenly rise and roil up and attack like a tsunami, kicking you in the stomach, tossing you around, sucking every breath from your body. It can pull you under, making you feel dizzy and sick to your stomach. Your equilibrium is disturbed. This thief called Grief has stolen your identity, security, peace of mind and purpose and replaced them with fear. There is fear in every decision you make. Fear in summoning the courage to go out in public. Fear that you will not survive this great loss. Fear that you will never stop crying. Grief is in partnership with fear, so keep reminding yourself that this is normal.

If you live alone now, you may not want to cook meals

for one person. You may forget to eat meals you have made. Your taste buds may be compromised so food tastes like sawdust. You may struggle with digestive problems such as nausea, queasy stomach, diarrhea or constipation. You may have a pounding headache that never seems to subside.

Your sleep patterns may have changed. You may sleep too much or too little. You may forget to breathe, and hold your breath for long periods of time. Sighing is the result. Practice this breathing technique: Inhale through your nostrils, push your tummy out, hold for six seconds, then exhale through your nostrils, holding your tummy in for six seconds. This relaxation technique helped calm me and improved my sleep patterns.

Your skills of concentration are limited, aren't they? If you don't write things down, they may slip your mind entirely. I forgot everything until I started carrying a little notebook with me. You may be getting lots of free advice from family and friends. While this advice is often (accidentally) inappropriate, sometimes it is sound and worth recording. I also wrote my daily tasks in this little book and tried to complete one or two tasks a day during the first eight months. Don't try to complete more than you think you can handle. Pat yourself on the back for being able to get out of bed and complete even a couple of tasks.

Some of your friends may be quite task-oriented. They can help with a couple of things right off the bat. Suggest they take the children for an afternoon or your dog for a long walk, to give you a break. Perhaps they could bring you dinner once a week or take you to medical appointments. Ask for their assistance with the paperwork involved with your loved one's death. If you don't ask, you won't get. Worse yet, if you don't ask, people who want to help won't know how and may feel that they're failing you.

Whether you are at the bottom of the mountain, in a wilderness or in a desert, you will find your way. Take a guilt-free "grief break." Give yourself permission to do something to take your mind off things, even for a few hours. My grief breaks usually took me out of town, to the theatre with girlfriends.

You, too, have friends, even if you wonder lately where they are. Why did they stop visiting or calling after the first month? What happened after the funeral when everyone went back to their normal routines? Where are all of the people who promised support and said they would "be there" for you, now that you need them? As I said, you have to *ask them* for help.

Some friends and family members can enter into your pain. Others cannot and will not. You may be a reminder to a friend that it is possible for him or her to lose a child, spouse or parent. They fear the label you now have, whether it's widow, widower, bereaved parent or orphan.

Monica was hurt when her good friends Jennifer and Mimi stopped visiting after her husband Jacques died. Seven months later, they finally blurted out to Monica,

I had many true girlfriends I could call on for support. Only one couple though, Becky and Al, stayed by me throughout the difficult weeks after Rhod died. Our other "couple friends" faded into the night. I made new couple friends (including my girlfriends' husbands) who were very supportive, such as Pat and Bob, and Ingrid and Roger. People will tell you to call them if you need anything, and that can be frustrating as you know you're unlikely, in the haze of grief, to take that initiative. It shifts the onus onto you, when you're already struggling. But you must call people. I knew I had to reach out for support, so I invited people to my home. I urge you to do the same.

"We can't visit you in your home because it hurts too much! We miss Jacques, too!" Selfish? Yes. Common? Definitely.

As I advised Monica, cast bitterness aside because it will eat you up and you are worth more. All people are in our lives for a reason, as we are in theirs for a reason. Remind yourself to be thankful for the time you had with this person, and try to forgive the fact that right now, he or she simply cannot support you. Cut your losses and move on.

No matter how often we see people, severe loneliness is inevitable at certain times. Jane felt it on weekends; Jill, during evenings. For me, early mornings were the worst because Rhod was a shift worker. I heard his key in the lock at six a.m. for several months after his death. I would awaken suddenly, sure that I had heard the front door open. I also missed him keenly when I came home from work in the evenings. I missed his snoring, even though I had hated his snoring. I wished I could hear it and be driven into another bedroom for a good night's sleep just one more time. This was part of my yearning phase. The yearning for what I had lost.

Don't mope and isolate yourself for long periods of time. The phone may not ring. Be proactive and make that call yourself. It is OK to have a quick "pity party," but don't stay down in the dumps for too long. Give yourself permission to stay in your pajamas for a few hours or for a day, eating chocolate and watching soap operas. Then pick yourself up, dust yourself off and get motivated to take on a new day.

EXAMPLE

Lela had to educate her friends about grief and bereavement. Friends would say, "I don't like to see you so sad. When are you going to be back to your old self? You used to be so much fun." Lela's hurt was really tough, and oh-so-painful. Her friends did and could not understand because they had not experienced the loss of a child. They could only imagine. We, the bereaved, have to be the teachers for our family, friends and co-workers. Lela was able to find strength through a support group and a couple of friends who walked alongside her gently, rather than taking her by the hand and dragging her through her grief. We have to teach others that all that is needed is a good listener who will patiently let you tell your story over and over until you believe it yourself. Get rid of the pressure of trying to return to your old self. That is not going to happen. You are forever changed and will have to recreate and rebuild.

When Jamie was 35, his dad died. He had been married to Jamie's mom for 44 years. She went through an extremely intense mourning process. Jamie was afraid of losing his mom, too, and kept saying to her, "You need to get over Dad! I want you back to your old self! It has been six months and it is time you got on with your life!" He was treating grief and mourning like an event instead of a process. With education and counselling, Jamie was able to verbalize his fear, thereby lessening the pressure on his mom and giving her permission to feel the pain of loss.

Incorporate the word "normal" into your language because what you are experiencing is normal. I promise you it is. The loss of your hopes and dreams, of your history and of your future with your deceased loved one has changed you in the blink of an eye. You are moving, however slowly, toward a new normal. You will see.

MINIMALIZING YOUR GRIEF:

Free advice: "You should sell your home now. It is too big for you." "You should go back to work" or "You should not go back to work." In my situation, because I was a palliative coordinator of volunteer services, my manager suggested that my recent bereavement might make me unsuited to the position now. "Don't worry; you'll get married again." "You have two other healthy children." "Be thankful your father lived a long life." "You should be grateful you had 60 years together. Hang onto your memories." "You will have more children." "A cure just wasn't meant to be." "At least he's not suffering anymore."

When Jill's son died, her physician said, "Now you must know how Mary felt when Jesus died!" When Sarah's daughter passed away of SIDS at 11 weeks of age, a friend said, "Well, you hadn't had all that long to get attached to her." Forgive and forgive and forgive again, but educate these people about how those statements make you feel. If you suppress your anger, it will deplete you of the good energy that you need at this time.

BEACON OF HOPE

Secondary losses can complicate your grief journey. Recognize that you are grappling with issues that can complicate your grief process and give yourself extra time to breathe if you're confronted by one or any of the following (and this is not an exhaustive list):

- You must sell your home for financial reasons.
- You fear living alone; fear for your safety.
- You have young children or ailing parents with needs that must be met.
- You and your deceased loved one were co-dependent.
- You care for your surviving children, parent, sibling.
- You are mourning a relationship you did not have with a loved one, and now never will.
- You have health-care issues of any sort.
- You can't reconcile yourself to the type of death: motor vehicle accident, homicide, suicide, workplace accident, sudden trauma.
- You need to move to a retirement home because your deceased spouse was your care-giver.
- You lack social support.
- You are geographically isolated.

CHAPTER 6

SWIMMING IN THE OCEAN — HANGING ON BY A THREAD OF HOPE

*D*on't fight the tumultuous waves of grief. Let them roll over you, or float along on them. You will eventually find a safe haven.

Realize that if you love with intensity, you will grieve with intensity. Mourning is going forth with those feelings and not fighting them. The pain sometimes will seem unbearable, so you need to take a grief break. Find a distraction. Take a trip away from your environment.

Meet friends for dinner or find solace and sanctuary in

your garden or your local park. Embrace your "alone time." Your memory and concentration may be not what they used to be. Reading may have been a joy to you but now you may read the same sentence or paragraph over and over and still not get the gist of it. Practice reading for 20 minutes, then listen to music for 20 minutes. Relax and take a deep breath; this will change!

You may mimic or be on the lookout for the symptoms of your deceased loved one. You may think you have cancer. You may suddenly find a lump or feel a tingling sensation you have never felt before. You may feel light-headed or dizzy. You may have shooting pains down your left arm and believe you're having a heart attack. It is not uncommon for the recently bereaved to go to emergency rooms or to see their physicians with their deceased love ones' precise symptoms.

You may or may not feel safe in your own home. You may be sensitive to neighbourhood noises – from people to lawn mowers to traffic – that didn't affect you before your loved one's death. You may suddenly find you're getting up three times a night to make sure that you locked and bolted your doors. Because of financial and other circumstances, you may have to move. Sandra and her husband Bill were living in subsidized housing with 24-hour care because of Bill's ill health. When he died, she had to move with just three weeks' notice. Her friends in the building had been a huge support and now she was dealing with this loss, too.

My home was my safety net. I was comfortable with my memories and I did not want to or have to move. Many people advised me to sell my home. "It is too big and too lonely for you now." "The memories must be difficult for you," was another refrain. Not so. I needed my memories. You have to go to the memories, good and bad, to get through the pain of loss. But it is in the sharing of these memories with others that you do your work of mourning. People will probably tell you not to make any big decisions for at least one year. After one year has passed, they may begin pressing you. I want to emphasize again that there is only one time frame in which you can make these decisions: *yours*. Do what is best for you. Listen to your gut.

Jane's self-esteem and confidence took a huge hit after her husband Sid died. A year later, she had difficulty functioning in her small community, worrying about what others thought and might say to or about her. It got to the point that she needed a new vehicle but was afraid to buy one in case she was judged. Little decisions became big decisions; moderate decisions became major decisions.

Stacy, a mother of two young children, bought a new car a month after her husband died. When her friend, Vera, was asked by a member of the community how Stacy was doing, before Vera could reply, the person said, "She must be doing great; she just bought herself a new car!" It was no one's business, but Stacy bought the car because she wanted a safer vehicle for her children.

Her rationale isn't surprising. When you lose a loved one, you may fear the loss of your living loved ones, and have increased anxiety about their safety. These feelings may stay with you for a few months or a few years. Realize that this is part of your journey. When those ominous thoughts come up, say to yourself, "I am not going to feel anxious. Worrying will do no one any good. I banish these thoughts!" I switched my mind to gratefulness instead.

Jean and her husband were married for 30 years. They lived and worked together. They did everything as a couple, to the point of co-dependency. When James died, Jean's adjustment was more difficult because of these circumstances. Half of her was missing. Her personal and professional life had revolved around James. She was his partner and wife. Now she was a widow, a term she hated, and worse yet, she was alone, having to cope with small decisions that snowballed into big decisions. She was afraid to initiate a conversation with the males in her community for fear of being talked about. She was afraid of laughing for fear of being judged. Jean found herself when she took a grief break and left her environment for two- or three-day trips with her girlfriends. Away, she didn't have a label and didn't have to look over her shoulder. Grief breaks are essential to a healthy grief and mourning journey.

BEACON OF HOPE

- Grief work is the hardest work that I have had to do.
- Take a break and don't feel guilty.
- Write day-to-day tasks in a purse- or pocket-sized notebook.
- Listen to your intuition and look after number one.

If things can go wrong after a loved one dies, they will. It seems that roofs will leak, faucets will drip, furnaces will go stone cold and cars will break down … these inconveniences become huge tasks to deal with. I know. I experienced these and they took a lot of energy and added a lot of stress.

One Saturday night, I had girlfriends over for dinner. We were eating in the dining room. Suddenly we heard a scratching noise in the living-room ceiling. We assumed I had bats, because I had returned home from vacation a few times to find the unwanted winged creatures hanging from my curtains. I shrugged it off for the weekend. On Monday, I called a local pest-control company.

Joe came over and, after checking the house, in the attic above the garage he found a mother raccoon with a young litter. Did I say at this time, "Why the hell me again?" I sure did! I could have screamed. I felt besieged by problems and did not want to deal with any more.

Joe told me that we had to wait a few weeks before he could try to safely trap the mom and her kits. I did not think I could wait; I felt like I was going crazy. I vented my frustration with my good friends Carolyn and Jon Newman, who are non-judgmental and great listeners. Jon told me that I could remedy the situation immediately. He suggested that I play ear-splitting rock music, with as much force as my stereo could muster, to drive out the mother and babes.

I took his advice. The volume was so loud that I had to leave my home. Several hours later, my neighbour saw Mrs. Raccoon and her wee uns exit my house and wind their way down my driveway. No, they did not return. My trick? I threw tons of moth balls up in the garage attic.

Before your loved one died, you could tackle these problems with confidence. You even chuckled about them or shared them as dinner-party anecdotes. Now, you may feel that having to deal with unexpected or even day-today issues is taxing and takes all your energy. Take a step back. Realize that we can't change our environment or unforeseen challenges – we can only change our mindset and how we react to them. Be gentle with yourself as you grieve and mourn and let yourself feel the extra weight of challenges you know you could have dealt with readily, in an earlier time. When you scale your mountain of grief and reach its pinnacle, you will be able to look back at these incidents and laugh about them.

Tips for surviving the storm of Loss

- Decide that you will survive and thrive but give yourself permission to take baby steps.
- Start off every morning by counting your blessings. Remind yourself of them throughout every day. Don't watch the news before bedtime.
- Spray your pillow with lavender. It's soothing.

- Go for a walk in early evening when the light is at its prettiest.
- Reach out and call a friend who is a good listener.
- Watch a funny movie.
- Join a laughter yoga club. Fake or forced laughter has the same benefits as authentic laughter and laughter truly is the best medicine.
- Write down your dreams and goals and take this opportunity to pursue them. Travel. Start Spanish lessons. Enroll in a dance class. Bungee jump. You know better than most that we all should have a dream list.
- Use the good dishes.
- Live in the moment. If you go to the past, don't linger. If you go to the future, just take a quick glimpse and come back to the now.

- Practice meditation.
- Write a grateful list daily
- Think positive thoughts.
- Read a paragraph, verse or phrase from an inspirational book.
- Express yourself through your journal.

BEACON OF HOPE

If you fight the waves of grief, you will get sucked down in the undertow to what lies beneath.

Go with your feelings of pain and you will float along with the waves. Befriend all these feelings and go with the flow. The intensity of pain will calm over time. You will know when you have turned a corner in your grief journey. Don't try to rush through it. It's not a race. The reward won't be a medal. Be patient with yourself and others around you. Envelop and bathe yourself in your feelings, then move forward taking baby steps. Teach those around you that you need their gentle hands and support now. Don't let pride get in your way. If need be, seek out a professional counsellor, minister or rabbi at a local church, synagogue, funeral home or hospice.

CHAPTER 7

THROW GUILT IN THE TRASH CAN

*I*t is human nature to feel guilt after a loved one dies, whether suddenly through suicide, homicide, a workplace tragedy or a motor vehicle accident, or if the death was anticipated. You will inevitably think of words that you now want to say to your loved one. "What if…?" "If only…" "I should have…" "Why didn't I…?" But guilt is a useless, energy-sapping, negative and draining emotion.

Yes, there is much that you wanted to say to that person but you didn't have the opportunity. The last words exchanged may have been in anger. You may feel cheated that you did not have a chance to repair the relationship before his or her death. You may feel guilty when you laugh. This is a natural reaction to loss. Having regrets or even bitterness about the parting is normal, but you must let these feelings go. If you internalize them, they will devour and destroy you. Release this negativity. Forgive yourself and others around you.

This soul work demands a lot of energy. It is important to explore, reflect and ponder – then it's even more important to let go. Allow this experience to be an opportunity to get to know yourself and the "new" you. For me, every challenge and transition became an opportunity for growth. For you, they can be, too.

Guilt may rear its ugly head because you are relieved that your loved one has died. He or she is not suffering anymore, or perhaps the relationship was not a good one. It is not easy to discuss these feelings with family or friends because of the fear of being judged or deemed a bad per-

Paula's best friend since childhood, Dee, died. One year later, Paula came to me for counselling. She told me about the lives they had shared together. Both married and had children, then grandchildren. When Dee was diagnosed with cancer, Paula was devastated. She spent many weekends at Dee's home, reminiscing about and reflecting on their lives, laughing, crying, and providing support to Dee and her family. Now, the void was huge in Paula's life. Her marriage was somewhat rocky and Dee had been the stabilizer in Paula's life. She felt guilty that she missed her friend so much. She was angry with Dee for dying because she now had no one to turn to for support. Dee had been her good listener, who did not judge when Paula vented.

son. Guilt may arise when a friend has died and you did not fully realize how important she or he was in your support network. Often people with whom we are in the closest relationships are not in our family tree. Whether family by blood or family by choice, if we love with a fierce intensity, we will grieve with a fierce intensity.

Later, when Paula's feelings were validated and normalized, she was able to grieve and mourn her best friend. She was able to remember and honour Dee and let go of the feelings of guilt, associated with thinking her husband should have been her soulmate.

Sara was 14 when her grandfather died. She was devastated. "Poppa" had played the role of dad, because Sara's parents were divorced and she had lived with her grandparents. Family and friends expected her to be strong and responsible but she started acting out. She became rebellious, hanging out with older teenagers. Counselling helped Sara and her family understand the role her beloved Poppa had played and her deep attachment to him. Sara is 19 now and is off to university, but she still misses Poppa.

Virginia's father died when she was 26. At one of the funeral visitations, she was complimented by several people on how strong she was being for her family. On the day of her dad's funeral, she broke down in tears. Several people admonished her, "You shouldn't cry now, especially on the day of the funeral!" She felt guilty and worried that she had disappointed her mother and other family members by being unable to maintain her composure.

Joan read Dr. Kubler-Ross's book and was upset because she did not feel "anger" when she thought she should have. She had somehow moved past that to acceptance. Penny, on the other hand, was angry for several years after the death of her daughter and wondered if she would ever move on to acceptance. She eventually did, but only when she was able to take her anger and use it constructively. Then, she memorialized her daughter by establishing a college scholarship for graduating students. In Penny's suffering, she found meaning and richness in life again.

The late psychiatrist and pioneer on death and dying, Dr. Elisabeth Kubler-Ross, outlined five stages of grief: denial, anger, bargaining, depression and acceptance. This model was never intended to be taken literally. Grief is an ongoing process and not linear.

Susan took on the role of mother to her own mother, when Susan was only seven years old.

Her mother suffered from manic depression. Mother assumed the role of daughter and Susan became the mother figure. Susan was 21 when her mom died. She mourned the relationship that she did not have and longed for the mom that she had wanted but never had. It was a relationship that was never to be. Ultimately, Susan decided to turn this loss into a positive. She asked her elderly neighbour, Barb, if she would take on the role of being Susan's surrogate mom. Barb was delighted. Do what works for you as the griever!

BEACON OF HOPE: Coping strategies

- Write a letter to your deceased loved one.
- Do self-talk that guilt is a useless emotion.
- Balance bad memories with good memories.

- Light a candle and say, "I love you," to your deceased loved one.
- Take a walk in nature and observe how the birds and animals interact.
- Validate the feelings that are unique to you.
- Seek out a mentor, minister, friend or counsellor.

BEACON OF HOPE

Feelings of guilt are natural in your grief journey. It is important to share these feelings, whether through talking to a friend or writing them down. It is just fine to have a ritual of writing a letter or letters to your deceased loved one. Feel free to burn the correspondence or to tear it up when it has served its purpose. Listen to your gut rather than your head. Give yourself the permission and the time to heal. Remember, it is natural and normal for the bad memories to surface within us. When that happens, bring up a good memory to achieve balance. That is important to our healing.

Honour the relationship that you had with your loved one. Remember that the only change you can effect is within yourself, but you can use strategies to help you heal and cope with your loss. A piece of you will die when your loved one dies. That is natural and normal. Confront your feelings, share them and let them gently go. You will have to revisit them time and time again. Don't live in the shadow of your grief. When you are ready, you will rebuild your life without your loved one. Your relationship will be one of memory, and even though you sometimes are fearful of forgetting, you never will.

Sorrow makes us all children again.

Ralph Waldo Emerson

Let mourning stop when one's grief is fully expressed.

Confucius

All my life I have tried to pluck a thistle and plant a flower wherever the flower would grow in thought and mind.

Abraham Lincoln

CHAPTER 8

EMOTIONAL ROLLER— COASTER RIDE

Grief is like riding a roller coaster. We want to get off, but we can't. We have to hold tight and make the full journey, whether we want to or not. It took me 18 months before I saw any light at the end of the tunnel after my husband died. It took me six years before I came to terms with the loss of my adult child.

My emotions were all over the map, charging up, hurtling down and thrusting me sideways. I would start one task, go on to another, and end up accomplishing neither. I would go from Point A to Point B and not know why. I went from room to room in my home, forgetting what I was looking for. You may feel like you are going crazy. You are not. Confusion is an offspring of loss.

You may feel that you can't deal with feelings of pain anymore but, fortunately or unfortunately, you will be able to. You may wish this craziness would subside because you want to move forward with your life without your loved one. You won't "get over it" in two months, as society's myth teaches us. You will "get over" your intense pain, eventually, but you will still have to learn to rebuild your life without your loved one physically beside you. And yes, that can still be difficult.

When I realized that I had to mourn Steven and Tate, too, after Rhod died, I knew that I was in for a rough ride and I certainly was. I sometimes questioned my sanity. There were times when I wanted to scream. There were times when I did not know who to grieve and mourn. It was overwhelming. That was one of the reasons for writing in my journals. I experienced too many different feelings crashing into each other in the same time frame. I would consciously plan to mourn Steven, then Tate or Rhod. I had to put the brakes on a bit. My mind was racing at a very high speed.

Several people asked me which loss I grieved more: my son, my granddaughter or my husband. This question put me on a bigger roller-coaster ride. I told them I was grieving all three and I can still see the stunned looks on their faces. One friend told me that going through her divorce must be worse than my going through my husband's death. She stated that at least death is final. I retorted, "You still have an opportunity to reunite with your husband or still see him physically in person if you so choose!"

Then there were the friends that told me, "Wow, you're bad luck!" when I hope they meant I was just experiencing bad luck, losing half of my family. This was not helpful. I learned to tell them, "This is my life journey and I can't change it."

I chose to be a survivor and a thriver, not a victim of grief. As the late psychiatrist and concentration-camp survivor Viktor Frankl stated in my favourite book, *Man's Search for Meaning*: "It is not that suffering will make you stronger but finding meaning in suffering will make you stronger."

BEACON OF HOPE

You don't have any energy to waste now. Step back and do the self-talk.

This journey is yours and yours alone. Embrace your pain and you will come out the other side healthy and full of purpose and courage. You, unlike many others, will know what you can endure. Don't push against the pain; that just makes the roller-coaster ride more terrifying. Learn to listen to your body, mind and soul. Free advice will be plentiful, but feel free to ignore it and do what's best for you during this difficult transition. Going through grief makes you feel like you are going crazy because you have lost control. Believe that this is normal, and trust me: Over time, you will regain control again. Actively work on your mourning, do your memory work, search for meaning in your loss, and make time for good nutrition, plenty of rest and exercise. You will develop a "new identity" and a "new normal" without your deceased loved one in your own time frame. All rides – good and bad – come to an end at some point.

CHAPTER 9

RISING FROM
THE ASHES OF GRIEF

*I*t may be easier said than done, but you can rise from the ashes and live a full life again without your loved one. Remember the phoenix. You will be forever changed by your loss, but you will be reborn. Support is a huge key to this healing journey. You may have to reach out for it from family and friends. Be around people who lift you up emotionally and who don't minimize your feelings of loss.

Seek out supporters that will "walk with you" on your journey and not "drag, push or judge" you as you scale the mountain of grief. This support must be ongoing, not just for a couple of months after your loss. If your child died, seek out and be around other bereaved parents. They are the best mentors. Unlike most of your friends, they *do* know what you're going through and don't have to "imagine" how horrible it is.

Often, the grief before us reminds us of griefs past, particularly if they're unresolved losses. When Rhod died, I not only revisited the deaths of my son and granddaughter, but other, earlier losses. One of these losses was when I was 15 years old. My boyfriend, Murdock, died in a motor vehicle accident. I was devastated but I internalized my feelings. When Rhod died and I started to consciously do my work of mourning, I was transported back to the day of Murdock's death. I knew that I had to revisit this tragedy because those past feelings overpowered my loss of Rhod. I was able to cast my mind back and write those feelings about Murdock's death on paper and then gently let them go. I also was able to talk to my friend and cousin,

Violet, who supported me when my high-school friend died. We went over the memory of Murdock's funeral, shared the sadness briefly, then released it. It is important to remember that you have to go back before you move forward. Many of us may have unresolved losses that will need to be revisited as we go through our current loss.

A part of us dies when our loved ones die; they take a piece of us with them. We lose a part of who we are or were as a person. You can reshape and rebuild your life, and learn to live and love again, as I did. We are forever changed by our losses and you will learn that that is all right. This acceptance takes time and what you do with your time is important. Be good to yourself. If you are a worry-wart, get yourself a worry box. Write down your worries daily and make a date with yourself a week later to re-read them. I assure you, 50 per cent will have been resolved and the other 50 per cent will now be meaningless to you.

Live your life in joy and triumph, not fear and trepidation. From the ashes of your grief and sorrow you will begin life anew and, if you choose to, you will live life fully in the gift of today. Don't anticipate more sorrow and pain tomorrow. Living marginally is not living life with meaning, in my estimation. The sun did shine for me again. The birds did sing for me, and life was good, but different. Grief work was the hardest work that I have ever done but when I made the decision to look after "me," that was the turning point for me. To do this, you will have to confront the challenges associated with your journey and believe that you will heal, survive and thrive again. Accept and learn that all of these transitions and challenges are new shoots of growth for us.

In my healing journey, I acknowledged that my loved ones had died, I assimilated these losses and I accepted them. This bereavement journey involved intentional, physical, psychological, emotional, mental and spiritual work to nurture myself. It is your responsibility to take charge, realizing that when the shock wears off, you may feel deep, gut-wrenching pain that you must embrace. Learn coping strategies to help you live well so you can live life to the fullest again, with your deceased loved ones in your memory and your heart.

BEACON OF HOPE

Equip yourself with tools to feel, heal and live again.

Physical

- Walk alone or with a friend.
- A hot bath with music and candles released my day-to-day stress.
- Working out at my local gym gave me energy and social time and a reason to keep moving.
- Neil Diamond music helped me dance with abandon – alone but joyful.

- I joined a formal yoga class and told the instructor why I needed extra tender, loving care.

- The sun kissed me for 20 minutes a day as needed.

- I revved up my diet with more antioxidants through more veggies and fruit.

- I pampered myself with a weekly massage for a few months, then bi-monthly and then monthly, until I had maxed out my late husband's benefits.

- I visited a local park and watched the birds and animals interact.

- I rested my body two or three times a day for 20 minutes, listening to music.

Emotional

- I practiced deep breathing exercises several times a day, thinking, "I am calm and peaceful."
- I shared my story and my feelings with two or three good friends who did not judge me.
- I listened to music I find calming: Yanni, Beethoven and Mozart.
- I reached out and hugged my family and friends.
- I petted and lavished attention on my two cats, who did not judge me or my feelings.
- I frequently phoned family and friends, long-distance
- I was aware of my feelings at different times during the day.
-

- I wrote notes and letters to loved ones, then burned my missives.
- I acknowledged my accomplishments and told myself out loud that I was proud of myself (self-talk).
- I acknowledged and addressed my fears and let them go.
- I recited daily affirmations and expressed thanks for what I had.
- I visualized thoughts of peace, acceptance and joy.

Mental

- I stated an affirmation out loud.
- I expressed my fears, thoughts and pain in a journal.
- I attended bereavement workshops, lectures and university courses.

- I read books and magazine articles on grief and bereavement.
- I listened to self-help tapes as I drove to appointments.
- I watched funny movies to boost my "sadness" immune system.
- I wrote "to do" lists and planned to accomplish two tasks a day.
- I wrote a list of goals and dreams with the intention that if I did not accomplish them, I would change them. Always have a dream.
- I planned on having a good day upon awakening.
- I thought positive thoughts and pushed away negative thoughts.
- I brought up good memories to counteract bad memories.
- I devised a plan to recreate and rebuild my new life.

Spiritual

- Believe in the power of prayer.
- Talk to a guardian angel.
- Visualize life as peaceful.
- Attend church services.
- Study other religions at university.
- Reach out and help others in the community.

Meditative

- Take quiet time to listen to a guided meditation tape.
- Visualize and write about the spiritual journey through grief.
- Join a book club or start one with friends.
- Start a laughter leader club (check out www.laughteryoga.com).

I have achieved growth and courage and purpose beyond my wildest dreams.

I didn't die when my loved ones died. I went through, rather than around, the door of pain to the other side. I experienced deep loneliness, and endured visceral pain with my head held high. Through my losses, I turned my sorrows into gifts to help others cope and heal. Growth can shine through your sorrow… Believe and it will happen! Tap into your gifts to give you strength in your deepest, darkest days. Realize that you will again feel the sun's warmth, hear the birds' sweet music and look forward to each new day with anticipation and grace, if you make that your choice.

You will survive if you believe. We have to do the work of mourning and, unfortunately, sometimes in the midst of our deep sorrow, another special person is wrenched suddenly from our life. Pat is a survivor and I admire her tenacity. She keeps going despite losing her daughter, her son and her husband within a two-year time frame. Yes, there are many moments when she feels that she can't put one foot in front of the other and yes, she does sometimes wonder if there's any point in going on. She is still an infant in her grief journey but she wants to survive and thrive. She has found reasons. She has reconnected with her church community, she is reaching out to others as they grieve and is the architect of a new "Pat," forever changed by her losses.

I am a changed person because of my losses. I loved the old me but I love the new me more.

I am more confident, positive and spiritual and, through helping others, I know that I am using my gifts. Public speaking is supposed to be traumatic for most people, but I am at ease and confident with it now. I know I have gained that strength and other traits because of my life – and death – experiences. I have dreams. I live in the moment!

My goal is to educate people about death and dying before they suffer a first significant loss or another significant loss. Always have a dream, no matter what your age is. If you don't achieve your dream in the time frame that you hope for, change the dream. Nurture your spirit and open your soul. Reach out to the universe. Ask and you will receive, but you have to *believe*.

BEACON OF HOPE

I was a rough piece of rock until I became a polished diamond. I became a diamond because of my loss experience and you will, too, if you believe! I look forward to each new day. I can't wait to see whose life I will touch and who will touch my life. I know that I will experience much more sorrow and transition in my lifetime, but I don't go looking for it. I know I can cope and deal with whatever is thrown in my path.

Your bereavement journey will cripple you for a while, but you will be able to walk, then scale and conquer that mountain of grief when you are ready and in your own time. Don't fear the work of grieving and mourning. Live life as you should and find meaning in your sorrow. Do as I did and turn your sorrow into gifts to help others cope and heal.

We are the educators because we have the experience and know the truth. It is our role to teach and show others that death is a part of every life journey. Good luck and God bless you as you embark on your bereavement journey. Be gentle and smile through your tears. The view from the top of the mountain is lovely and it will be yours one day, too.

WRITING OUT OF THE BLUE

Journal

ACKNOWLEDGE

ACCLIMATIZE

ASSIMILATE

ACCEPT

AFFIRM

Loss breaks us open for potential growth. The telling of our story over and over until we are able to integrate it within us strengthens us. Our stories are interconnected like the rivers. You don't have to feel alone in your sorrow. Just look at the landscape of your life.

Grief and mourning are like the tides, high and low. The tide goes out and the tide comes in. In high tide, you will feel intense pain and in low tide, diminished pain. Waves pounding on the shore will take your breath away as you stand in a tide's wake. The sound of waves rushing to shore is soothing and calming, yet painful. When you swim in the ocean, do not fight the waves or you will get sucked in by the undertow. It is the same way with your bereavement journey. Go with the waves and you will float along. Go with your feelings of sorrow and do not let fear be the victor.

The pain of grief can be endured and *must* be endured to live life fully again, yet differently.

This experience will split you wide open. Yes, you will suffer deeply, but you will also be freed to examine and reflect upon who you are as a person. Your goals and dreams will have changed, but I assure you that you will find new goals and dreams if you dare to believe.

What you accepted and looked forward to before your loss is different now. Priorities are muddled, expectations lowered, and you find yourself fearing what can be a confusing and difficult journey.

Muster up the courage to express your feelings of loss and pain through writing. It is only when you take those feelings of pain, bring them forward from inside and go public with them that your healing will begin to take root. To heal you must feel. Start practicing here and now, with this journal. Make it your journal.

Remember that if you loved intensely, you will grieve intensely.

In *Man's Search for Meaning*, Viktor Frankl stated that, "It is not that suffering makes us stronger but finding meaning and purpose in our suffering that makes us stronger." I believe that to the depths of my soul.

Audrey's Five As for a "New Normal"

My foundation for scaling the mountain of grief consists of what I call Audrey's Five As. They will help you overcome what I went through and you are no doubt going through in the wake of the loss of your loved one: losses of self, identity, joy, meaning and self-confidence; changes in health, personality and lifestyle; and for some of us, challenges with our physical, emotional and financial lives. These are but a few of the things we can find ourselves confronting in the aftermath, and these are the Five As that will help steer you through turbulent times.

1. **Acknowledge** the death of your loved one. That is, say the word "died." Don't avoid discussing it and don't use euphemisms to try to talk around it or soften the blow. Your loved one died. Acknowledge that.

2. **Acclimatize** yourself to the deep feelings of grief and mourning. Accept that pain is a part of your loss journey. If you push against the pain, your journey will be more difficult. Accept and go with your feelings of loss.

3. **Assimilate** your new life. Learn to pick up the pieces and rebuild it without your loved one. This process is often done in baby steps and always in your unique time frame.

4. **Accept** that you will be forever changed by the death of your loved one. You will never get over your loss but in time you will gradually learn to live without your loved one and go on the journey of developing a "new normal" without him or her.

5. **Affirm** the life you lived before and find yourself living now. Through affirmations, you will be able to flourish, rebuilding and reshaping who you are as a person. Consciously plan to live life again to the fullest, with your loved one in your heart but not at your side.

Audrey's Tips to Survive and Thrive While Scaling the Mountain of Grief

1. Don't forget to breathe. When I was grieving, I had a tendency to hold my breath and as a result I was prone to sighing. Learn yoga breathing techniques to assist you. Let us practice now: Sit in a comfortable position, close your eyes, breathe in through your nostrils to the count of six, hold for a count of six, then exhale through your mouth to count of six.

   Practice this technique for two minutes. I must learn to breathe because

   _____

   _____

   _____

   _____

2. I must start my day with feelings of "thankfulness," even though this is difficult to do right now. This technique will help bolster my physical and mental immune system.

   Today, I am thankful for _____

   _____

   _____

   _____

3. My bereavement journey has so far been one of solitude. I feel alone, sad, empty and desperately miss

   _____

   It is important to take time to reflect on your loss, but the support of loved ones will get you through the difficult times.

I think_____,_____, _____

_____, _____, will be good listeners,

non-judgmental, compassionate, and will not drag me

through my grief but will walk with me on my journey. I

must reach out to_____

_____

_____.

4. Realize from this moment that there are no set
   "stages," as some models suggest. Your feelings are
   yours and yours alone so don't feel that you must go
   through denial, anger, bargaining, depression and
   acceptance in a systematic pattern. You may experience
   all or none of these emotions within a one-minute time
   frame. Be aware that this is emotionally draining and
   taxing for your psyche.

My feelings are all over the map most days. Today, I feel

_____

_____

_____

_____

5. Make a plan to survive and thrive despite your huge
    loss, and despite feeling miserable, lost or over-
    whelmed. I made my "To do list" every day for 18
    months after my husband, Rhod, died. My hopes and
    dreams died when he died, but I decided to generate
    and commit to new hopes and dreams with the plan of
    moving forward one day at a time, perhaps alone, but
    healthy emotionally, physically and spiritually.

    I have to think about surviving without_____

    because I_____

SCALING THE MOUNTAIN OF GRIEF:
The Power and Strength of Belief

My hopes and dreams died when _____

died but now I must make new ones.

1. _____

2. _____

3. _____

4. _____

5. _____

6. _____

7. _____

8. _____

9. _____

10. _____

Some of these hopes and dreams are scary without

you, but I need them so I can _____

_____

_____

_____. And I know you would approve of them,

especially number ___ because _____

6. Remember that we are human beings and not one of us
   is perfect. Don't elevate your loved one to sainthood
   after his or her death. Ask yourself why you are putting
   your deceased loved one on a pedestal.

   Am I putting _____on a pedestal?

   Why? _____

   I remember the good times we had, such as _____

   _____

These memories sustain _____

_____

But there were human flaws, as there are with any of

us, such as _____. I even miss those traits,

but yes, _____, you were human.

7. Recognize that guilt is a useless and draining emotion but entirely natural on your grief journey. If unresolved issues arise after the death of your loved one in the form of guilt, take these steps. Write your feelings in a journal, write a letter to your loved one and use the ritual of burning the letter or burying it afterwards, or talk openly about the feelings with your pastor or counsellor. It is natural for "What if ..." and "If only ..." to arise and nudge you to reflect.

I know it is natural to feel guilty and right now, I feel

guilty because _____

Sometimes I feel guilty when _____

_____.

But I am going to try to _____

_____

_____

I need to share my feelings with _____

_____ and I know that I will feel

better because _____

_____

I miss you so much because you _____

_____

I am so angry at _____

_____

_____

_____

8. Balance the bad memories that arise within you with
   the good memories. It is normal for unpleasant memories to rise to the surface first. Prepare yourself for the
   good, the bad and the ugly memories that you experience. You will eventually accept all of them as steps forward in your grief journey.

   I remember the last conversation with_____and I

   was angry/resentful and we _____

   _____but I will balance that by

   remembering the good time when _____

   _____

   _____

_____

and I also remember when _____

_____

9.   Give yourself permission to be a child again. Take baby
     steps as you grieve and mourn. Don't try to run when
     you can only crawl. You may feel like a vulnerable child
     surrounded by the unknown or danger, with all sorts of
     safety issues. You need to feel nurtured, pampered and
     supported during this difficult time. I needed support
     for years after my losses. You will, too. Remember to
     reach out for support and don't feel shame or failure.
     Needing reassurance is normal.

     I feel very vulnerable, weak and I am not myself when __

     _____

     _____. I will have to do self

care and reach out to _____

_____

_____ I will have to develop a

new normal because _____

_____

_____

10. Don't feel guilty when you laugh. Laughter is the best
    medicine for your overall health. Join a laughter club,
    watch funny movies and be around people with a sense
    of humour. Fake it 'til you make it!

    I want to laugh again but when I do laugh, I feel

    _____

    _____

    I must work at not feeling guilty because _____

    _____

    I am so afraid of _____

_____

_____

11. You will feel a sense of joy again… just imagine and believe!

Joy will creep into your life for a second or two and gradually stay longer.

It has been such a long time since I felt joy. I remember an occasion when_____

_____

_____

When I think about _____, I know that I will feel joy again.

12. If you let yourself feel the pain, bring the pain from the inside to the outside and you will heal. Healing is feeling pain and letting it go.

This pain is so hard to bear. Sometimes I feel _____

_____

_____.

The loneliness is _____

_____.

I feel so alone when _____

_____

_____

13. You will have to recreate and rebuild a world without your loved one physically present but remember he or she will always be in your memory and heart. Try to imagine what your world will be like now, without your deceased love one.

I try to imagine sometimes what it would feel like without you and I_____

_____

_____.

Sometimes it is too painful to think about and I _____

_____

_____

14. Find strength in spirituality. Find solace in nature, art,
    music or community.

    I know I must start a routine, so as of today, I must _____

    _____

    _____.

    This helped me before when I was going through a

    crisis: _____

    _____

    _____

15. Dig deep within yourself and bring forth the strategies and resources that helped you cope and heal through previous losses. You grew through them. Take a leap of courage to go within and explore those times.

I remember when I was_____years old and _____

_____

The ways I coped then were _____

_____

_____

16. Befriend your grief journey. Don't be afraid.

I have to stop being afraid of my grief journey. This is

the normal reaction to my losing_____

_____.

The stress will lessen if I _____

_____

_____.

I will take a grief break because _____

_____

or I can plan to mourn_____for thirty/sixty

minutes and then I will_____

_____.

17. Self-care is very important to your healing. Write your thoughts, hopes and fears in a Feelings Journal. Write, but don't read what you have written. If you read, you will experience the pain twice and it will stop you from writing again. Instead, write, then look in a mirror and repeat the mantra "I am number one now" over and over until you believe it.

I will set a goal of writing daily about _____

_____

_____. This is important for my healing. I know that

I have to feel to heal. It is so difficult because I _____

_____

_____

I won't read what I have written because I don't want to

feel my pain twice. I will turn the page as I write. I am

having a hundred thoughts go through my head at the

same time and these are my thoughts _____

_____ How am I going to survive

without you?_____ My family and

friends don't understand what I am going through.

_____ I must tell_____ how I really feel

inside because_____

_____

_____

18. Embrace the loneliness and emptiness and remember that these feelings will ease and lessen as you turn corners in your grief journey. If you live alone now, leave the radio or TV on for company when you return home. Judy adopted a dog from the Humane Society and this joyous ball of fluff gave her a reason to jump out of bed in the morning and motivated her to exercise.

It is so lonely and empty without_____. The void is

_____.

I will _____to help me with loneliness

because _____

_____

_____

_____

_____

19. It is all right to cry. You won't get a medal for being strong. You will cry tears so long and so hard that you may wonder, "Will I ever stop crying?" Give yourself permission to release feelings of pain and don't apologize. Release emotions to heal.

My friends and family tell me that I have to be strong,

so it is difficult when I_____

_____

_____

_____

Some friends let me cry while others like _____

_____

so I must find three good listeners so I don't wear then

all out when I am _____

20. Remember the times that tears rise to the surface and you push them down inside of you. This may happen in the workplace, at public functions, or with family or friends. Repressing tears takes lot of energy that you may not have. Crying cleanses the soul but remember to drink lots of water to replenish those tears.

Tears rise up within me and I _____

_____

_____

_____

_____

21. "Grief" is your emotions and "mourning" is going public with those emotions. Circumstances may stop you from mourning, as they did with Rachel. Her husband died and she had three young children. She arranged

with her workplace to take Fridays off for the first year after her husband's death, so she could consciously do her work of "mourning." She poured over her memories, sometimes with a friend, and other times alone. Every other Friday, she visited her counsellor.

I know the importance of taking a grief break because

_____

_____.

So I will mourn when _____

and I will feel good about that mourning.

22. Start new traditions and rituals if that is what you need. Respect the old ones but create new ones. It is OK to keep the old traditions. Do whatever works for you.

I plan to continue with these old traditions _____

_____

_____

But I also plan on starting up these new traditions

_____

_____

All of these traditions, new and old, will _____

_____

_____

_____

23. Remember: Don't be all things to all people now. Your
energy level may be low, your nerves may be frayed,
and your patience and tolerance may be at all-time
lows. Respect and acknowledge those feelings. Go with
what works for you and don't feel shame or guilt.

I am not the same person as I was before _____

died but everyone expects "the old me" to resurface.

I have to take care of me now because _____

_____

_____

I must explain to_____how I have changed and

why now I have to develop a new normal without

_____

24. Make time for yourself and remember to make yourself
    number one. Book a pedicure, manicure, massage or a
    new haircut. Go golfing or play squash. A makeover
    might give you a much-needed boost.

    I have to take care of number one now so I can _____

    _____.

    In the next few days, I will do these things to try to revi-

    talize or pamper myself _____

    _____

I am not the same person so I will change_____

_____

and that is okay.

25. Remember to get lots of sleep, rest and proper nutrition. Rest your depleted body two or three times a day,
for at least 20 to 30 minutes. I would put on a Yanni CD
and lay on the couch. This may feel like learning a foreign language, but do it. You will gather strength to do
day-to-day tasks. You are not being selfish. Release
those negative thoughts.

When I go to bed, I _____

_____

_____.

When I rest, I _____

Now I have to consciously use the aid of music or_____

to help me nurture my mind, body and soul. I think that

music that might help me would be _____

_____.

26. Spend time with people who care about you and do not
judge or give you free advice. If you are feeling low and
vulnerable, don't be around people who will suck the
energy out of you. You need to conserve energy now.
Be around people who will lift your spirits and nurture
you. Remember: You are not the caretaker to your
friends now; you are the one with special needs who
requires TLC.

My role has changed because _____

_____.

My friends still expect me to _____

_____.

My energy level is _____

_____.

I will tell my family and friends _____

_____

because_____

_____

_____

_____.

27. Join a bereavement support group in your community.
    You won't feel like the only person who is a bereaved
    parent/ spouse/ sibling, etc. You will make new friends
    who understand much of what you are experiencing.

    I need to be around people who experience some of the

    same _____

    _____

_____

so that I can be supported and understood. I have to be conscious that I may have a caregiver personality and be cautious when I join these groups not to take on others' pain or minimize my feelings of loss.

I will validate my feelings of _____

_____

_____

and not compare them to others'. We are all individual and as unique as our thumbprint.

28. You may experience anxiety leading up to the anniversary of your loved one's death. The actual anniversary day, you might well get through without too much anxiety. You may dread not only the day but the month when your loved one died. For several years, I disliked Tuesdays and Saturdays, August, September and February.

I dread the day my_____died. I can deal with it

better if I prepare myself. I know that the anticipation

of the anniversary or birthday is more difficult. On the

day of _____I will make plans to_____

_____

_____.

I know that I may have to change old rituals, so I will ___

_____

_____

_____.

29. Don't give yourself a timeline such as "three months" or
"one year" to get to a certain point in your grief journey. Your timeline is yours and yours alone. We are all
unique human beings with unique grief and loss experiences. Discard the myth about the "firsts." For me, the

second year was worse than the first, because I was in shock for the first six or eight months following deaths. Reduce the pressure on yourself and say, "I will take one moment at a time and in my speed and timeline."

I am not going to set a timeline for grief or compare mine to others because _____

_____

_____

_____

30. You may feel you have lost your past and your future when your loved one dies. Where has your history gone? Where is the person who was so integral to it? When you are ready, you will rebuild a new future but you will not ever forget your history or past whether you lose a child, spouse, parent or best friend.

I remember when I married/met/gave birth to

_____. We were together for_____ years. I

want _____ more. My life was_____

_____

_____.

Now it feels _____

_____

I know that I will feel again _____

_____

_____

I must practice self-talk to help me stay positive in

difficult moments, hours and days.

31. Your goal is to get over your intense pain and learn to live with the loss of your loved one. You will never get over or forget your loved one. You will experience joy again so just believe and let your journey unfold. Visualize "joy" and try to experience feelings associated with it.

JOY is _____.

When I think of these images or memories, I remember

joy: _____.

I will get over my intense pain and have more moments

like that because I plan to _____.

I must reach out for support because if I don't, my

journey will be _____

_____

_____

32. If you have several losses within a short time frame, as I
    did, your grief journey may be even more complicated
    and confusing.

    My losses in the last ___ year(s) are _____,

    _____,_____,_____

    I am so happy that_____in my life and I remember

    _____I am afraid of forgetting

    _____but I know that it is just fear and grief is

    fear! I am afraid of forgetting _____because

    he/she _____

    _____

    _____

    But I could never possibly forget _____

    _____

or _____

_____

or _____

_____.

33. Don't beat yourself up! If you love hard, you will grieve
and mourn hard. If the attachment to your loved one
was minimal, you may not feel intense pain. You may
experience the loss of a relationship that did not exist
between you and your deceased loved one. This is
normal.

I never thought I would feel this much pain when

_____died. I don't want to feel _____

_____.

I should be able to move forward but I am having

difficulty because _____

_____

_____.

My relationship with_____was one of _____

_____.

I wish my relationship was_____

_____

_____

34. Learn to live your life in the gift of today. We only have
this day and, often, really only this one moment. You
will learn through your losses that we only have this one
moment, so the value of the moment is higher. That is a
gift stemming from grief.

I must learn to live my life in the gift of today because

_____

_____the strategies that I am going to use are

_____

_____

35. Just when I think that I am doing well, I am back to feeling the deep sorrow I did a few months/year(s) ago. This
is just fine and natural and I must tell myself this.

Seventeen years after my son Steven's death, I experienced all of the pain and relived the day he died and
that of his funeral. It was agonizing. However, I realized
that this was normal so I did not push away those feelings. Instead, I expressed them and then was able to
move forward.

I will move forward and then _____

_____

but I know that this is part of my healing. I will not be

fearful. I will go with the emotions of _____

_____

_____

that I am experiencing this moment.

36. You may experience anxiety inside, but try to keep it together on the outside.

    We have a tendency to "act" and smile in public, when we are crying inside. When anxious feelings well up, practice deep breathing. When going to appointments, allow yourself more time to prepare and to get to these appointments.

I was in one mode for months____slow! This is okay and

normal. I do feel_____

_____

_____.

My energy level is low because grief work is very drain-

ing and takes all of my energy. So I must conserve

because_____

_____

_____.

37. Be aware of changing seasons. You may feel more vul-
    nerable and sensitive to your environment.

    Today is the first day of summer and I feel _____

    _____.

Today is the first day of spring and I feel _____

_____

I noticed autumn today and I feel _____

_____

Winter has arrived and I feel _____

_____.

I must remember that if I didn't love, I wouldn't feel so

_____

_____.

38. Your timeline in dispensing of personal items is your
   timeline. I gave family and friends personal items of
   Rhod's. A year later, I was able to give his clothing to
   local agencies but I had to give some of mine, too.

   That is a letting go. Don't feel that you need to do this
   task immediately.

It took Carolyn three years after her husband died before she started going though his clothing and giving these precious items to different agencies. Sometimes, you learn more about your deceased loved one in this process. Carolyn didn't realize what a pack rat Jon was and she laughed and cried as she sorted through his possessions.

Sammy's daughter's room is exactly the same as it was when her daughter died in a tragic accident. A year has passed, but she finds comfort in going to Susan's room and going to the memories. Only Sammy will know when the time has come to part with Susan's belongings.

I know that I have to go to the pain to get through the pain and part of this ritual is going through _____ personal belongings and going to the memories of

_____. It is normal

that I feel unprepared to tackle this. Maybe I'll know I'm

ready the day I _____

_____.

39. It may be difficult for some of you to have photos and
memorabilia of your loved one displayed in your home.
For others, this is a comfort, as it was for me.

This is normal! I made photo albums for my grandchildren when their grandpa died.

This was healing for me and also important to my
grandchildren's healing.

I must _____

because_____

_____

40. It is fine to hang onto symbols and rituals to help you cope and heal.

I love angels and I found great comfort in them in my darkest days. My collection of angels from family and friends still gives me strength and peace.

Butterflies are the symbol of the cycle of life and still provide hope and strength for me. I collect rocks and stones on my travels and when I am stressed or anxious, I rub a stone I keep in my pocket, to calm me down.

I have several pots of rocks and stones. Every single one of them is different in texture, colour and size – just like you, me and our bereavement journeys.

The rituals and symbols that are soothing for me are

_____

_____

I find comfort in _____

_____

_____

41. I remember the day that I awoke and I heard the birds
singing, I saw the sky was blue and I smelled the sweet
flowers in the air. All of my senses awakened to this new
day. I had turned a corner at the 18-month mark after
my husband's death and a feeling of peace was within
me. It took me six years after my son died to find even
one minute of peace. This is part of what convinced me
that grief is a journey, and we can learn how to scale
that mountain one tenuous, rocky step at a time.

I remember when_____

_____

_____

_____

I will scale that mountain because_____

_____

_____

42. There is so much to miss and yearn for when your loved one dies.My Steven was taller than I am and had the habit of patting me on the head when he visited me. I miss not hearing my mom's knitting needles clicking as she lay on the couch knitting socks during our many visits. I miss my Rhod's crazy sense of humour. This is natural and normal and to be shared.

I miss _____

_____

_____

I wish I could _____

_____

_____

I yearn once more to _____

_____

_____

43. Secondary losses can be monumental and impede your bereavement journey. It may be as simple as eating alone at home or in a restaurant or going to the theatre alone. It could be more far-reaching, as was Elise's, as she did not have a driver's license when her husband died. Sheila is legally blind and her husband was not only her caregiver but also her eyes. When he died suddenly of a brain aneurysm at age forty-nine, Sheila was forced to sell her home and move to an apartment complex against her wishes. For me, living alone for the first time in forty-eight years was terrifying and took many months of adjustment.

My secondary losses are _____

_____

_____

_____

_____

44. I remember having difficulty with going from saying
"we" to saying "I" when my husband died. For months
and months in conversations I started with "we." This is
natural and normal. Over time I consciously started
conversations with "I." That is when reality set in.

I will practice saying "I" instead of "we" because

_____

_____

_____

_____

45. The fear factor may be intensified when your loved one dies. I was fearful of losing my surviving children when Steven died. I feared that my dad would die when my mom died. It is important for children/adolescents to talk about their fear of loss. Betsy, age six, was afraid of going to bed to sleep at night for months because the message she received when her Aunt Betty died was "Aunt Betty has gone to sleep." Betsy slept with the aid of a nightlight for a year and the true reason only came out when she attended a children's support group.

I fear that _____

_____

_____

_____

_____

_____

My child's/children's fears are _____

_____

_____

_____

_____

I will share my fears with my spouse/parent/ sibling/

children/friend because _____

_____

_____

_____

_____

46. Losing a loved one makes us feel vulnerable, sensitive,
    insecure and often makes us suffer from low selfworth.

It is important to try to remain positive despite the pit-falls. My memory was compromised to the point where at times I felt like I was losing my mind. When my anxiety level increased, my memory decreased. Be aware that you are in control. Calm your mind and you can calm your body.

Today, I am more aware of my feelings and I feel _____

_____

_____

_____

_____

It is important to be calm because_____

_____

_____

_____

47. Get yourself a "Worry Box." If you have always been a worrier, your worries after the death of your loved one may spiral out of control. Sadie worries about yesterday, tomorrow and today. She is exhausted and expending all of her good energy. As her worries pop up, she writes them down and makes a date to read them one week later. Half of them have resolved themselves and she wonders why she took on the other half in the first place. This strategy works because she is taking her worries, bringing them outside of herself and letting them go.

I worry about _____

_____

_____

_____

_____

Today I am worrying because _____

_____

I am not going to take on the worry of _____

_____

_____

_____

48. It is natural to feel a twinge of jealousy or even anger
    when you see couples holding hands or laughing and
    enjoying each other's company. I know I did. Jim did,
    too, when his wife Fran died. Rena felt anger when her
    friends complained about their teenagers. Her son Brad
    had died .

    I know that it is okay to feel _____

    _____

    _____

I need to express these feelings of _____

_____

_____

49. Have the courage to enter into your pain of loss. Grief work is soul work and it requires walking toward the deep pain, embracing it, working though it and emerging on the other side with more gifts, as I did. If you become stuck and are not moving forward, it is important to seek the guidance of a counselor, pastor or support group.

In my reflection today I _____

_____

_____

I must suspend and be still and _____

_____

_____

I have learned in my bereavement journey that _____

_____

_____

_____

50. Finally, and for some, most frighteningly, your belief
    system may be called into question. Will was an avid
    church goer, but when his wife died, he stopped attend-
    ing. He blamed his God because He did not heal Blanche.
    Maria became more aware of her surroundings when
    her daughter Kim died. She found nature to be very
    spiritual and healing. I found comfort in my church
    community and in nature. This kind of thing is individ-
    ual to each of us as humans.

    My belief systems consist of _____

    _____

    _____

Before _____died, I_____

_____

_____

Now I_____

_____

_____

_____

Those are my tips for healing.

What are yours? You will discover many more as you scale the mountain of grief. And yes, you will scale it. All the best, and be gentle with yourself as you journey through loss.

My tips to heal are _____

_____

_____

_____

_____

_____

_____

_____

_____

_____

_____

_____

_____

_____

_____

SCALING THE MOUNTAIN OF GRIEF:
The Power and Strength of Belief

Creating Meaningful Funeral Ceremonies: A Guide for Caregivers, by Alan D. Wolfelt, PhD.

This guide assists caregivers in creating special ceremonies for loved ones and helps them during the grieving process.

The Fall of Freddie the Leaf: A Story for Life of All Ages, by Leo Buscaglia, PhD.

This children's book is suitable for all ages. It tells the story of Freddie and his companions and how their leaves change with the passing seasons. It warmly illustrates the balance between life and death. I often read this little book at the beginning of a workshop.

Care of the Soul: A Guide for Cultivating Depth and Sacredness in Everyday Life, by Thomas Moore.

I read this book in the first year after Rhod's death when I was searching for answers about myself. It taught me to take care of my soul in a society that Moore says is

AFTERWORD

I hope that *Scaling the Mountain of Grief* has been
and comfort to you and that you return to it ofte
find solace and reassurance that your journey is unfoldi.
precisely as it should: in *your* way and timeframe.

I thought I would share a few books that were of great
assistance and inspiration for me, in case you want to
continue reading as you scale that mountain.

Man's Search for Meaning, by Viktor Frankl

I read this book at least ten times. I was inspired by
reading Frankl's story of survival in a concentration camp.
If he could survive, I surely could, too. Sometimes I would
only read a line or a page. His words brought me hope and
support.

full of obsessions, addictions, violence and loss of meaning in our lives.

When Bad Things Happen to Good People, by Harold S. Kushner.

The author wrote this book after his fourteen-year-old son died. It is a life-affirming work that talks about the struggle with hard times and personal pain. It is filled with compassion and hope.

The Art of Happiness: A Handbook for Living, by the Dalai Lama and Howard C. Cutler, MD.

Learn how to defeat anger, anxiety and discouragement and live a happy life despite suffering.

Blessings,

Audrey

READER FEEDBACK

How Did This Book Affect Your Grief Journey?

I Want To Hear From You.

Share your stories and experiences of loss with me. I will make every possible effort to respond with a personal note. Please write to:

Audrey Stringer

c/o A String of Hope Inc.

P.O. Box 22037

Sarnia, Ontario, Canada

N7S 6J4

Or contact me via www.astringofhope.com

ORDER FORM

Check your local bookstore for *Scaling the Mountain of Grief* or *Get Over It!*

Order by:

Telephone: **519 331-1728**

E-Mail: _____

Web: _____

Mail: Audrey Stringer c/o A String of Hope Inc.,
        P.O. Box 22037, Sarnia, ON, Can, N7S 6J4

PRICE: $20.00 CAN/US

(please note that shipping and handling costs are extra)

Canadian residents add 5% HST

Please make cheques payable to: **A String of Hope Inc.**

Ask about our discount orders on quantity purchases for your organization.